Florida's Prehistoric Stone Technology

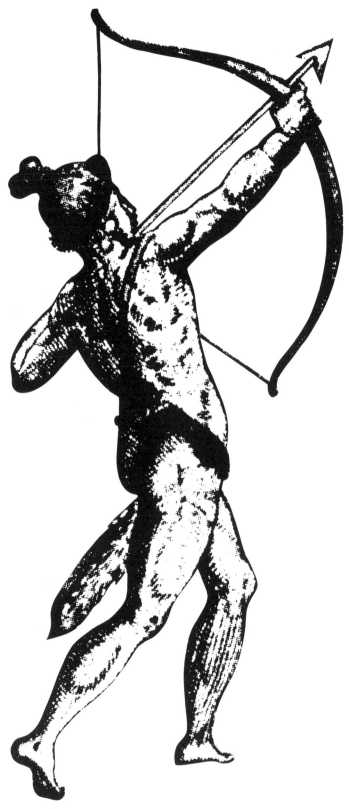

From *The Youth at Their Exercises*, engraving by le Moyne

Florida's Prehistoric Stone Technology

Barbara A. Purdy

A University of Florida Book
University Presses of Florida
Gainesville

University Presses of Florida is the central agency for scholarly publishing of the State of Florida's university system. Its offices are located at 15 NW 15th Street, Gainesville, FL 32603. Works published by University Presses of Florida are evaluated and selected for publication by a faculty editorial committee of any one of Florida's nine public universities: Florida A&M University (Tallahassee), Florida Atlantic University (Boca Raton), Florida International University (Miami), Florida State University (Tallahassee), University of Central Florida (Orlando), University of Florida (Gainesville), University of North Florida (Jacksonville), University of South Florida (Tampa), University of West Florida (Pensacola).

Library of Congress Cataloging in Publication Data

Purdy, Barbara A
    Florida's prehistoric stone technology.

    "A University of Florida Book."
    Bibliography: p.
    Includes index.
    1. Indians of North America—Florida—Imple-
ments. 2. Stone implements—Florida. 3. Indians
of North America—Florida—Antiquities. 4. Florida
—Antiquities. I. Title.
E78.F6P87   975.9'01   80-24726
ISBN 0-8130-0697-X

Typography and design by University Presses of Florida
Printed in the United States

To Richard D. Daugherty

It's hell in the field.

Contents

List of illustrations

List of illustrations

Preface

In prehistoric Florida, as elsewhere, many items of the material culture could not have been manufactured without the development and refinement of stoneworking techniques. To appreciate this point it is necessary only to consider that, whereas in modern societies nearly all material items are made by or of metal, in most North American prehistoric societies nearly all items were made by or of stone, the hardest, sharpest, most durable, and most plentiful substance available. The technology involved in producing chipped stone tools is as old as mankind, and although it represented such an important and essential industry for so long in human history, it was readily abandoned when metals were invented. Stoneworking techniques fell into disuse and were forgotten after metal began to perform tasks originally accomplished with stone. During the Age of Exploration, Europeans discovered New World peoples using tool-making methods long ago discarded in Europe. Since there was no way for the explorers to relate the significance of these "esoteric" practices to their own worlds, their written records include only condescending and uninquiring reports of the aborigines' manufacture and use of stone implements. Since Florida chert has continued to have little if any economic importance into the twentieth century, it is likewise often difficult for us to recognize and evaluate its economic value to and its influence upon prehistoric society.

For over a hundred years archaeologists have recognized that stylistic differences in stone implements are important indicators of time period and geographic location, but only since the middle of the twentieth century has the field of lithic technology emerged to suggest how stone remains can be used to interpret past human behavior.

I do not believe we appreciate the important contributions made by prehistoric stoneworkers to modern technologies. In their search for suitable raw material, they became the world's first geologists, developing methods that would later be used in mining metal ores and gem stones, and they learned to recognize and use to advantage such natural properties as fracture characteristics. As this information was passed on, each generation modified and refined existing techniques and developed new techniques as they adapted to increasingly complex cultural and environmental challenges. Gradually, the physical, structural, and compositional components of many rock types came to be recognized—at least intuitively. Stoneworkers probably were the first chemists when they observed, perhaps accidentally, that changes occur in rocks when they are exposed to heat. Thermal alteration of silica minerals can be beneficial or detrimental, depending upon how heat is applied. The precise and controlled application of heat to induce beneficial changes in stones may have been a vital step before ceramic, plaster, glass, and metallurgical techniques could be developed and added to the cultural inventory. The importance of attaining and controlling high temperatures can be appreciated best by considering that even today mankind has still not yet achieved the thermal technology necessary to produce nuclear fusion.

In three major areas our understanding of the past can be enhanced by studying how prehistoric peoples used stone to cope with their environment. The first of these is the technology of primitive manufacturing processes. Chipping flint is a process of subtracting or removing material—a "reduction" process. For that reason it is possible to find artifacts in all stages of manufacture at stone outcrop work sites, and thus it is possible to determine step by step how the tools were produced. To discover how the artifacts were made and how that manufacturing process evolved over time, it is not enough to look just at finished products; observations of unfinished artifacts, revealing the stages of the production process at that time, are needed. For example, the sophisticated spearheads seen in museums represent the end product of manufacturing techniques that had been developing for more than two million years. To state that flint *was* used in a given era because all sorts of chert implements have been recovered is of less archaeological significance than being able to describe the techniques employed at that time to shape the flint. The tool-making techniques reveal more about the technical level of an ancient society while stylistic evaluation of the finished products probably tells us more about the age or period of the tools of manufacture.

Second, we study stone remains to learn what specific purposes the implements served. Stone tools perform four functions: pounding, scraping, cutting, and piercing. It takes but little training to recognize the implement used for each of these tasks; but in the absence of other preserved items of the material culture the archaeologist is challenged to discover what was actually pounded, scraped, cut, or pierced. The stone remains of a culture often provide the only evidence of the activities calling for the stone implements' manufacture.

Third, the classification of the stone implements by type, date, use, and place of origin adds to our understanding of early people. The past becomes clearer if specific specimens can be recognized as belonging to a specific time period or geographic area. Even more meaningful is the discovery that certain types of implements belong to a specific time period and thereby provide a means of determining comparative social development with other time periods. Stylistic differences in stone implements provide the prehistorian with a means to determine what processes stimulated a change both in the technology and culture of a prehistoric society. Geographic boundaries for tool types can be ascertained by stylistic differences and the information used to draw significant conclusions about regional variations in cultural patterns.

Although many types of artifacts usually perish in Florida because of the wet, moist climate and acidic soils, stone implements have

Preface

been recovered in abundance from all cultural periods. Florida provides an excellent opportunity to study stone remains because there are many chert (flint) sources that were utilized for thousands of years by early Florida inhabitants. The total technology involved in efficient conversion of a piece of stone into a finished tool depended greatly on locating and securing the suitable raw material. Through experience and intuition early Floridians obviously knew how to do this, but acceptable modern-day interpretations of prehistoric practices cannot be based on assumptions alone.

Scientific investigations employing instrumental analyses and microscopic examinations and attempting to duplicate stoneworking techniques have been conducted. These studies have revealed the chemical, physical, and structural properties of Florida cherts, leading to three significant gains in knowledge of primitive Florida stoneworking technology. (1) Weathering studies have led to a better understanding of prehistoric environmental conditions. (2) Use-wear studies by magnification and by comparison of Florida stone artifacts with stone implements still in use by, for example, the Australian aborigines have led to better understanding of the ways in which early Florida stone tools were used. (3) Replication studies have identified specific problems faced and overcome by early Florida stoneworkers.

Another investigative technique of modern science is thermoluminescent dating. This technique takes advantage of the thermal alteration aspect of primitive technologies and provides an accurate, absolute date when the altering of such specimens occurred. Accumulating such data, scientists can establish absolute chronologies and better evaluate cultural development across cultural or geographic boundaries.

This book is intended for three groups of readers: students of prehistory, that they may expand their understanding of the relationships between a people's early and later technological history; the people of Florida, that they may enhance their knowledge of a fundamental state resource and its use by the state's early residents;

and especially lithic technologists, in the hope that they will find here information applicable to other regions.

More than fifteen years of study of stoneworking technology has led me to write this book. My initial interest was stimulated about 1963 at Washington State University by Dr. Richard D. Daugherty after he had attended the first lithic symposium in Les Eyzies, France, which stressed ways stone remains could be used to reveal human behavior patterns in extinct cultures.

In 1967 I learned that little was known in Florida about the state's chert sources or their prehistoric use and it appeared that I could make a contribution to Florida archaeology by analyzing the stone remains and the technology that produced them. In 1969 I attended the first Stoneworking Session at Shoshone Falls, Idaho. (It was conducted by Don E. Crabtree and funded by the National Science Foundation.) This experience shaped the direction of my professional career. Learning to manufacture chipped stone implements, I gained valuable insights into problems encountered by primitive craftsmen. In addition, Don Crabtree's heat experiments with silica minerals led to my interest in thermal alteration.

In completing this book I have benefited from the assistance of many persons. I am indebted to colleagues in the University of Florida's College of Engineering, Department of Geology, and Department of Physics, particularly Drs. Genevieve S. Roessler, David E. Clark, Henri Van Rinsvelt, Byron Spangler, Frank N. Blanchard, H.K. Brooks, and E. Pirkle. Laurie M. Beach spent hundreds of hours compiling numerical data. Helen Bates appeared one day as if by magic and volunteered to illustrate the book "just to get the experience." A majority of the photographs were taken by Rob Blount, of the Florida State Museum, whose expertise and skill are apparent. Kay Purington, also of the Florida State Museum, provided photographic darkroom services and photographed many of the illustrations. Annette Fanus and Sharon Parr contributed many hours of typing and proofing. Without their help this book would still be in

Acknowledgments

a rough draft. Having had access since 1967 to the Florida State Museum—the collections, workspace, equipment, and cooperative museum personnel—I am grateful for the support of the museum curators, especially Dr. William R. Maples.

Since archaeologists often depend on "local lore" resulting from longtime amateur observation, George Neal, Alvin Hendrix, and Benjamin Waller have my special thanks for their willingness to share their important observations with me.

The Container Corporation of America, whose home office is in Chicago, Illinois, underwrote the costs of my excavations on their timberlands in north-central Florida. Because of the company's generosity I was able to conduct investigations that provided valuable information about quarry sites, and the analyses of some of these findings from these sites are included in this volume.

Although most of the book's conclusions resulted from my own observations and experiments, I nevertheless owe a debt to all those colleagues and associates who challenged and influenced my thinking throughout the years, in direct communication and while reading their works. I acknowledge with gratitude their contribution to the strengths of this presentation while I claim the weaknesses for myself.

Don E. Crabtree died November 16, 1980. Lithic technologists have lost a good friend, a stimulating colleague, and a brilliant mind. He could have answered so many questions I neglected to ask.

ONE

Early Florida Stone Implement Makers

They make their arrowheads from the teeth of fish and from stones which they cleverly fashion.

(Laudonnière 1975:11)

Laudonnière's comment is one of the few available historical accounts that even mentions stone (and it is possible he was referring to the Indians of Charlesfort, South Carolina, not to those of Florida). Nor is it certain that the following statement from the de Soto narratives was made about the Florida Indians: "The arrows are made of certain reeds like canes, very heavy and so tough that a sharpened cane passes through a shield. Some are pointed with a fish bone as sharp as an awl, and others with a certain stone like a diamond point" (Robertson 1932:37). This account also says that Indians from northwestern Timucua towns, having been captured by de Soto and kept in chains, at night "would file the chain off with a bit of stone which they have in place of iron tools" (p. 65).

Although the foremost authority on the Indians of the southeastern United States, John Swanton, lamented the fact that no early writer left a description of flint chipping (Swanton 1946:544), we are able to draw one conclusion about Florida stonemaking from the writings of Laudonnière and from the de Soto narratives—namely,

1

that some sixteenth-century Florida Indians manufactured and used stone implements.

Since the manufacture of spearheads and other stone implements, except for gun flints (Clarke 1935; Oakley 1972:7), was not part of sixteenth-century European technology, it is not surprising that historic documents from that era contain so few descriptions of the use of stone in early Florida cultures. Instead, we learn that arrows were tipped with wood, cane, hard sections of palmetto, tips of deer horns, turkey cockspurs, viper's teeth, spines of stingrays, tails of horseshoe crabs, animal bones, bird bills, fin bones, fish teeth, and fish scales, particularly those of the great brown spotted gar. Although it is impossible to make out the material with which they are tipped, spears and arrows are shown in le Moyne's drawings (see frontispiece).

As early as 1565, the Indians of Florida were using "piked pointes of kniues, which hauing gotten of the Frenchmen, broke the same, and put the points of them in their arrowes heads" (Markham 1878:53). From the documents we also learn that piercing, scraping, cutting, and pounding tasks were accomplished with shells, animal bones, and cane.

On the coasts of Florida, where most Europeans made contacts with the indigeneous people, there are no natural outcrops of flint or other hard rock except in the Tampa Bay area. When the French built Fort Caroline in 1564, the structures were made "with much terreplein of earth and fascines which is the fortification of this land, there being not a stone for a landmark in all of it" (Bennett 1964:154). If, by then, the interior had been explored and settled, the historic accounts might read quite differently. Evidence that the Europeans—at least their principal commanders—did not make explorations inland lies in the Menéndez statement, "We have not gone inland and therefore we have not seen any large towns, although there are many Indians and boys" (Bennett 1968:159).

Outcrops of high quality flint materials that were used extensively to fashion chipped stone tools occur in the central highlands of Florida. One historical account verifies this. Laudonnière states that

2

Saturiba, the cacique, or chief, who ruled the Fort Caroline area, was allied with Potano, the cacique of the area near present-day Gainesville. Potano was "a man cruel in war who had one thing particularly over the great Holata Utina, namely the barrages of the hard stones with which he armed his arrows" (Bennett 1964:174).

Archaeologists often rely heavily on historical records to provide information not preserved in tangible form: they are, however, in a position to supplement the written word by documenting the prehistoric use of stone with products from systematic excavations.

Thousands of recovered projectile points and other chipped stone tools manufactured from Florida chert contradict the implication of the historical accounts that stone tools were rare or nonexistent. In some parts of Florida so many stone tools and so much chipping debris are found that one might conclude that the state was densely populated in prehistoric times. I suspect, however, that people of yesterday, like those of today, wasted their plentiful resources. Oakley (1972) tells us, for example, that in Australia a native knapper "requiring a new knife will visit a traditional quarry and will perhaps strike as many as 300 flakes before he obtains what he considers to be a suitable blade. The rejects and waste-flakes are left on the working floor while the single satisfactory blade is taken away." Furthermore, the artifacts represent the accumulation of thousands of years of cultural debitage.

Chert was an essential raw material to Florida's early inhabitants, but it has not yet been studied thoroughly by modern students of archaeology. This situation may exist partially because, in the twentieth century, Florida chert has been of little economic importance and has generally been considered a nuisance. For example, chert overlays blocked access to more valuable limestone, and chert proved to be very hard on equipment in the crushed stone industry. In addition, the higher cost of extracting, hauling, and processing chert made it noncompetitive with other kinds of rock.

In the early twentieth century flint rock mining companies were located in Ocala, Leesburg, Williston, Morriston, and High Springs. Florida limestone formations contain various amounts of chert.

Stone Implement Makers

During limestone mining these silica-bearing particles must be separated from the limestone. The particles are then crushed to sizes suitable for use in concrete aggregate. Large amounts of chert also occur as residual boulders in areas where the original limestone has been weathered away. Crushed chert is sometime used as railroad ballast and in construction of jetties. Small amounts of uncrushed chert are used as building stones in the construction of structures (*Third Biennial Report,* Florida State Board of Conservation 1939). The concrete industry considers chert to be a deleterious substance: fine silica particles react with alkalies and, if present in quantities over 10 percent, produce harmful effects because silica is subject to considerable changes in volume. Chert can be used, however, in the asphalt industry without problems. Once a common building material, it is used less and less as the cost of stone masonry becomes prohibitively high (Southern Standard Building Code 1973; William Wisner and Byron Spangler 1977:personal communication).

TWO
Stone Tool Typology

. . . an object found in an archeological site is in reality
an historical document of past human action.

(Hole and Heizer 1973:202)

The word *type* refers to a particular kind of artifact (e.g., a Clovis point) "in which several attributes combine or cluster with sufficient frequency or in such distinctive ways that the archaeologist can define and label the artifact and can recognize it when he sees another example" (Hole and Heizer 1973:201).

The concept of type

Classification into types is a way to systematize descriptive data so that specific statements can be made about time and space relationships, techniques of manufacture, and functions of artifacts. Problems do sometimes arise in distinguishing one type from another. Since type categories are based on ideal or perfect forms, the ideal is seldom seen. In categorizing deviant specimens it may be found that one type grades into another, making a confident assignment to a specific type difficult. If the classifier is "a lumper," he will designate a single type with notations about the variations, much as the biologist designates species and subspecies. If the classifier is "a splitter," he will name a new type for each variant attribute he considers important. The latter method of classification (empirically derived, convenient, or designed) is arbitrary, imposed "by the classifier on the objects without consideration of the purpose the object may have served its maker. [On the other hand] discovered types are . . . 'real' and reflect forms that are assumed to have been culturally significant to their makers" (Hole and Heizer 1973:204).

Projectile points and other formal tools that required a mental template and a progression of manufacturing steps for their completion, which resulted in patterned, recognizable shapes, obviously are easier to identify than objects such as hammerstones. In the attempt to classify objects by age or place of origin or function, the distinction between "found" and manufactured implements is especially relevant: one flint hammer looks pretty much like another no matter where it was found or what it was used to batter, making it difficult to determine its age and origin.

Stone tool types

In Florida, because the moist climate and acidic soils have not preserved carbon-containing artifacts, it is difficult to establish absolute chronologies (with the exception of the limited number of specimens that can now be dated by thermoluminescence), and because of the lack of sequential geological information, it is difficult to establish reliable relative chronologies. Amateur collectors have recovered from rivers most of the known Paleo Indian artifacts; in fact, the best examples of all Florida's stone implements are held in private collections. Because stone artifacts have mostly been surface finds and because of the difficulty in establishing local chronologies, the chronology assigned to the prehistoric stone industries of Florida, particularly those of early periods, is based on typological similarities to stone remains from areas outside of Florida. Time periods of stone tool assemblages are uncertain unless found with implements receptive to positive classification. Although a stone tool kit can be postulated for each major period in Florida, implements such as hammerstones are difficult to subdivide typologically. They were probably used during all periods but cannot be positively assigned to the earliest periods.

The descriptions of the implements given on the following pages are not the final word about the chipped stone tool industry of Florida since point types and tool kits for each geographic area and each time period are still to be studied. When this information becomes available, it will be possible not only to recognize assemblages accompanying each point style but also to determine what tools were used in specific ecological settings. So far, I have drawn no final conclusions. This story of the primitive tools of Florida is primarily descriptive and comparative. Large quantities of data must yet be amassed for a definitive interpretation of how stone implements were used to meet the challenges of the culture and the environment. For example, before we may conclude that some implements were repeatedly resharpened and thus altered, we must have an adequate number of samples of the original version and an adequate number from every stage of modification.

The report considers other implements in addition to points, whose importance in lithic technology has heretofore received too much emphasis considering how little is known about them. Certainly they are the most diagnostic delineators we have; but they did, after all, perform only fairly restricted tasks. Researchers have tended to ignore or minimize the importance of such tools as scrapers, hammers, knives, and burins.

The classification of time periods used in this study follows fairly closely accepted chronology for the Paleo Indian, Late Paleo (or Transitional), and Preceramic Archaic periods. The terms *Early Ceramic* and *Late Ceramic* are my own time designations, used here only for convenience in discussing the stone implements of those periods.

It is not within the scope of this work to discuss, except in a general way, the broader cultural developments associated with stone tool kits. Certainly the stone tool industry should be integrated eventually with other cultural components in order to better represent the total society, but a great deal more information, which can be learned from replication studies and studies of use and wear, is necessary for a better understanding of a whole culture.

7

Stone Tool Typology

Table 1
Designated time periods used in this book

Time period	Approximate number of years ago
Late Ceramic period	500–2,000
Early Ceramic period	2,000–4,500
Preceramic Archaic period	4,500–9,000
Late Paleo period	9,000–10,000
Paleo Indian period	10,000–12,000

The objects chosen to illustrate tools from the five time periods were selected because research indicates that these specimens are "typical" representatives of a given class of artifacts.

Paleo Indian period

Projectile points

Projectile points are characterized by edge-grinding near the base, which is ground, concave, and unstemmed. The points are usually thin with excellent workmanship and generally fairly large sized, ranging from 7 to 10 centimeters in length with an average length of 3 to 15 centimeters. Florida has several Paleo Indian period point types, all fitting the above description but varying considerably in appearance (Bullen 1975:54–57) (fig. 1). They have been recovered primarily from rivers and springs, particularly in northern Florida (Waller and Dunbar 1977) (map 1, p. 60). Problem-oriented research of the Paleo Indian period is needed to determine if the points occur as extensively in other locations as they do in the Florida waterways.

The most numerous Paleo Indian projectiles found in Florida are Suwannee and Simpson points. Slight shape differences occur among examples of both Suwannee and Simpson points, but they are not great enough to justify new type names. Suwannee points appear to be quite uniform in size, but the Simpson points' dimensions vary tremendously (fig. 2a, b). Many hundreds of Paleo Indian projectile points have been found in Florida. Several hundred of these were recovered from approximately a two-mile stretch of the Santa Fe River and over fifty were found in the Oklawaha River. Paleo Indian

8

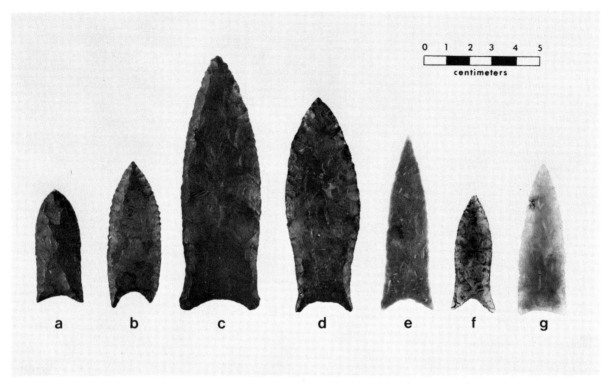

Figure 1. Projectile points of the Paleo Indian period: *(a)* Clovis, *(b)* Folsomlike, *(c)* Suwannee, *(d)* Simpson, *(e)* Tallahassee, *(f)* Beaver Lake, and *(g)* Santa Fe.

points are also fairly numerous in the Wacissa, Aucilla, and Waccasassa rivers (see map 1, p. 60, for additional locations). It is believed these points were hafted to thrusting spears and used to hunt the now extinct large Pleistocene mammals (Bullen 1975:2).

Although drills have been recovered from other Paleo Indian sites in North America, the drill shown in figure 3*a* is the only known Florida drill made from a modified Paleo Indian projectile point. The base of the specimen reflects a late Paleo characteristic. It was probably hafted, but the barbs are as smooth as the tip, suggesting that the implement might have been used unhafted and that the barbs functioned like the tip to accomplish the task being performed. It is sometimes difficult or impossible to distinguish between manufacturing attributes (e.g., ground base and barbs to facilitate hafting) and utilization features (e.g., tip smoothed and polished from drilling or perforating). The drill in figure 3*a* weighs 5 grams and is

Drills

9

Figure 2. *(a)* Suwannee and *(b)* Simpson points of the Paleo Indian period. (Note the uniformity in size of the Suwannee points and the variation in size of the Simpson points.)

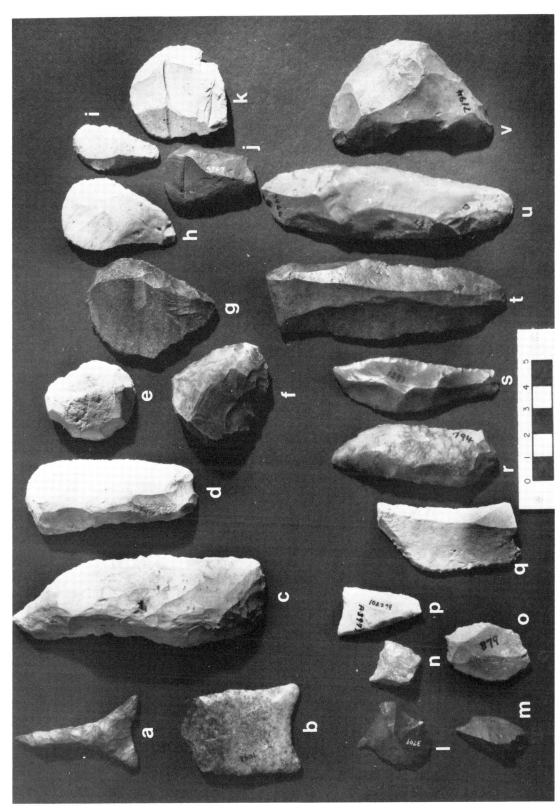

Figure 3. Stone tool kit of the Paleo Indian period: (a) drill, (b) hafted end scraper made from broken point, (c) Hendrix scraper, (d) snub-nosed scraper (oblong), (e,f) snub-nosed scrapers (triangular), (g,h,k) miscellaneous end scrapers, (i,j) thumbnail scrapers, (l,m) gravers, (n,o) scrapers with graver spurs, (p) spokeshave with graver spurs, (r,s,t,u) blades, (q,v) miscellaneous scrapers.

4.8 cm long, 3.0 cm wide at the base, and .7 cm thick. The steepest angle—about 90 degrees—is present on both sides just below the tip.

End scrapers made from points

End scrapers are probably modified Paleo Indian points that broke either in the process of manufacture or during use. The broken edge of the Suwannee point illustrated in figure 3*b* was pressure flaked to form an angle of 50 degrees. The specimen weighs 18 g, is 4.7 cm long, 3.1 cm wide, and .8 cm thick. Goodyear et al. (1968:91) discuss similar artifacts. Paleo Indian hafted end scrapers are not found in abundance in Florida (also see fig. 4).

Blades

Blades and numerous specialized implements made from blades are found in Paleo Indian complexes throughout North America. The following description of true blades is from Goodyear (1974:58).

One of the best definitions of true blades published, and the one followed in this study has been offered by Bordes and

Figure 4. End scraper.

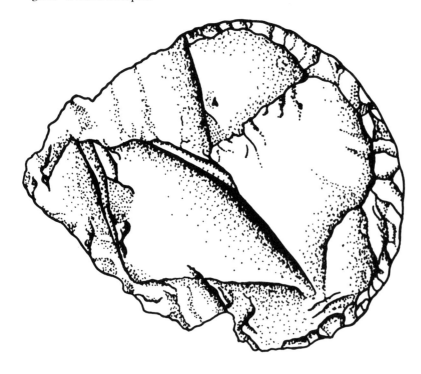

Crabtree from their flint-knapping experiments: "On the dorsal
side of the blade there should be two or more scars of previously
removed blades with force lines and compression rings indicating
that force was applied in the same direction as blade
detachment." In addition to this criterion, it is implicit that the
blade flakes will usually be twice as long as they are wide and
the blade margins fairly parallel. The cross section will be ". . .
plano convex, triangular, subtriangular, rectangular, often
trapezoidal, and on the dorsal face, [there will be] one or more
longitudinal crests or ridges" (Bordes and Crabtree 1969:1).
These cross sections are necessary in the detachment of blades or
other long flakes since the force of detachment must have ridges
to follow on the obverse face of the flake or what was the
exterior surface of the core."

Blades are the hallmark of the European Upper Paleolithic period
and have antecedents in the Mousterian and perhaps even the late
Acheulean periods. Many of the tools made on blades described for
the European Upper Paleolithic are found also at sites in North
America. Examples of complete blades are illustrated in figure 3r, s, t,
u. Their weights and measurements are: r = 21 g, 7.1 cm long, 2.4
cm wide, 1.1 cm thick; s = 9 g, 7.2 cm long, 2.3 cm wide, .5 cm thick;
t = 33 g, 10.3 cm long, 3.3 cm wide, 1.0 cm thick; u = 35 g, 10.9 cm
long, 3.1 cm wide, 1.0 cm thick. Figure 3r differs from the others in
the (length × width) ÷ (thickness × 100) index, which is .15 for r
whereas s, t, and u have an index of .33, .34, and .34, respectively.
The greater relative thickness of specimen r probably reflects a
different function from that of the others. Close examination reveals
that it was used as a scraper on both edges and perhaps as a chisel
at the tip. The proximal end is unmodified and the striking
platform and bulb are large. The other blades pictured were used
as knives and possibly also as scrapers. The presumption of use as a
knife rests on the observation that both faces of the long edges
exhibit small step and hinge fractures that have been reported to
occur when cutting certain materials (see for example, Tringham

13

1974:171–96). The distal ends, especially of *s* and *u,* may have been used as chisels and perforators or gravers. I see no indication that these blades were hafted.

Thumbnail scrapers

The specimens shown in figure 3*i* and *j* and in figure 5 are similar to those described for a number of Paleo Indian sites in North America. These included the Shoop, Bull Brook, Reagan, Stanfield-Worley, Eva, St. Albans, Hardaway, Thunderbird, and Russell Cave sites. Typologically, 3*i* resembles the chisel end scraper B-3 illustrated and discussed in Cambron and Hulse (1973:5), while 3*j* is similar in shape to their rectangular end scraper B-2 (p. 4) and is similar in angle of the distal end to their triangular end scraper B-1 (p. 3). The scraper illustrated in figure 3*i* and figure 5 was recovered at the Johnson Lake site (Bullen and Dolan 1959). The artifacts from this site are primarily Preceramic Archaic but include also some specimens typical of the Paleo Indian period.

Figure 3*j* was found in the Santa Fe River. William B. Roosa

Figure 5. Thumbnail scraper: *(a)* side view, *(b)* top view.

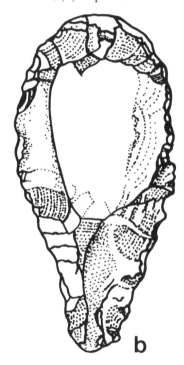

a   b

(Mason 1962:263–64) mentions that snub-nosed end scrapers are not found at Western Clovis sites but are present at other sites yielding fluted point (i.e., Folsom) and plano complexes. A tentative conclusion, therefore, is that the thumbnail scraper is part of the late Paleo Indian and of the Late Paleo tool kits. It is not known why the thumbnail scraper is not present in the early part of the Paleo Indian period since numerous publications dealing with the European Upper Paleolithic (Bordes 1968:156, 176, 194; Oakley 1972:30; and Tixier 1974:28) show it predating Clovis findings in North America.

The specimen illustrated in figure 3i weighs 3 g and is 3.7 cm long, 1.7 cm wide, and .6 cm thick. It has a very small, ground, striking platform. I believe it was made on a truncated blade by very careful uniform pressure flaking at the distal end and at both edges near the base. The angle of the pressure-flaked portions is about 50 degrees. I believe that it was not hafted because it shows use on both edges as well as on the distal end. All of the use was from the ventral toward the dorsal surface, as is apparent from numerous very small step fractures that partially obscure the pressure flakes. The specimen is entirely unifacial.

Figure 3j weighs 9 g and is 3.9 cm long, 2.6 cm wide, and .6 cm thick. The angle of the distal end is 90 degrees; the angle formed by both edges is about 50 degrees. The tool shown in 3j has a larger striking platform than i, indicating that it was intentionally struck farther back on the core to obtain a more massive piece. This fact, plus the difference in angle of the distal end, suggests that 3i and j did not serve similar functions. However, j's angle might have become steeper through repeated use and resharpening.

Spokeshaves are described by Goodyear (1973:39, 1974:50) and Bullen and Beilman (1973:6). The specimen illustrated in figure 3p weighs 5 g and is 3.5 cm long, 2.0 cm wide, and .6 cm thick. It appears to have been made from a blade, but the bulb and platform have been removed. The implement is primarily unifacial with a slight amount of flaking on the ventral surface. It has been pressure flaked to form an angle of 75 degrees at the distal end and a

*Spokeshaves
with graver spurs*

somewhat lesser angle at both edges. It bears a close resemblance to the thumbnail scraper, but it has not been reported as part of the stone tool assemblage for Paleo Indian sites in North America. Its placement in the Paleo Indian period, therefore, is tentative, yet Goodyear reaffirms that it may belong there. Goodyear (1974:50) suggests that the tool was hafted because of its small size. Hafting provided mechanical force permitting the use of greater pressure. A similar statement could be made about the thumbnail scraper. Close examination of the specimen illustrated reveals dulling of the lower edges suggestive of hafting.

Goodyear (1974:50–51) defines a spokeshave as any unifacially retouched concave edge suitable for scraping or shaving of narrow convex surfaces such as bone. The graver spurs are effective for slotting and grooving, and they should exhibit some battering or polish. This could not be detected on the specimen illustrated. These implements are fairly common and widely distributed in Florida. They are mistakenly labeled as very small Clear Fork gouges in Bullen and Beilman (1973:20).

Scrapers with graver spurs

Specimens similar to those shown in figure 3n and o have been found at Lindenmeier (Roberts 1936), Stanfield-Worley (DeJarnette et al. 1962:73), Hardaway (Coe 1964:75), Reagan (Ritchie 1953:252), Bull Brook (Byers 1954:348), Williamson (McCary 1951:14), Debert (MacDonald 1968:93), Rose Island (Chapman 1975:137, 140), Brand (Goodyear 1974:46), and various sites in Arkansas (Morse 1973:36). In Florida, these implements have been recovered at Bolen Bluff (Bullen and Wing 1968:94), the Nalcrest site (Bullen and Beilman 1973:1–22), and other locations, including the Santa Fe River. Figure 3n weighs 4 g and is 1.2 cm long, 1.9 cm wide, and .9 cm thick. Figure 3o weighs 6 g and is 3.6 cm long, 2.5 cm wide, and .5 cm thick. The angle of the scraping edges is about 65 degrees. There is considerable variation in the shape and size of these tools. The "typical" specimen resembles a short thumbnail scraper with a spur, but less typical specimens seem to have functioned similarly. Both *n* and *o* are unifacial and do not appear to have been hafted.

Implements similar to those pictured in figure 3*l, m,* and figure 6 occurred at least 40,000 years ago at Mousterian sites in the Old World (Bordes 1968:105, 107) and are described as part of the Paleo Indian stone tool assemblages at the Lindenmeier, Debert, Bull Brook, Rose Island, Brand, Stanfield-Worley, Thunderbird, and Reagan sites in North America approximately 10,000 years ago. Cambron and Hulse (1973:14, 17) have categorized these tools as Graver D-1, Chisel Graver D-2, and Uniface Borer 1-2, based on differences in manufacture and function. Goodyear (1974:53–57) follows a similar course. Tools comparable to those found at the Poverty Point site in Louisiana have also been found in Florida.

The graver shown in figure 3*l* weighs 3 g and is 2.9 cm long, 2.1 cm wide, and .9 cm thick with a spur about .4 cm long. The left side of the projection was formed by using a method similar to the

Gravers

Figure 6. Graver.

0   1   2

microburin technique of the European Upper Paleolithic period (Tixier 1974:17). The specimen was made from a thinning flake. The technique of making burins is explained in chapter three. In addition to its function as a graver, all its edges, except the proximal end and striking area, have been used for cutting or scraping or both. The implement shown in figures 3*m* and 6 weighs 3 g and is 3.2 cm long, 1.6 cm wide, and .9 cm thick. The projection is about .4 cm long and was formed by pressure flaking on both sides. The specimen was made from a short, thick blade or blade-like flake. There is no evidence of use other than as a graver tip. A nearly identical object was recovered at the Bull Brook site (Byers 1954:348). Neither 3*l* nor *m* appear to have been hafted nor do they exhibit any intentional modification except for the formation of the graver tip.

Hendrix scrapers Hendrix scrapers occur in fairly large numbers in Florida and has been reported as part of the Paleo Indian stone tool assemblage at the Shoop and Bull Brook sites (Witthoft 1952; Byers 1954). Bullen (1958) and Bullen and Dolan (1959) picture these as part of the artifact recovery at the Bolen Bluff and Johnson Lake sites in Florida, and Warren (1973) discusses an identical specimen found in St. Petersburg, Florida.

The specimen shown in figures 3*c* and 7*a, b, c* is considered typical. It weighs 87.5 g and is 10.4 cm long, 3.7 cm wide, and 2.2 cm thick. Measurements were made on a sample of 33 of these tools (fig. 8) with the following results: weight 37.0–257.9 g, length 7.8–16.2 cm, width 3.1–6.1 cm, thickness 1.7–4.0 cm. Twenty-three of the 33 weighed 60–120 g, 26 were 8–12 cm long, 28 were 3–5 cm wide, and 30 were 1.5–3 cm thick. All specimens were used as scrapers, but 5 had been used for piercing or cutting also. Both Witthoft and Byers describe the implements as side scrapers but 24 of the Florida specimens showed use around the entire circumference. The most intense use on 20 specimens, however, had been on the left edge of the distal end (tip). The shape varied: 4 ovate, 20 ellipsoid, and 9 triangular. All flaking had been done by

18

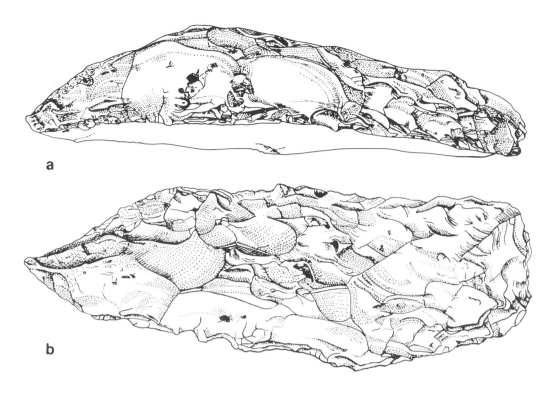

a

b

Figure 7. Hendrix scraper: *(a)* side view, *(b)* top view.

Figure 8. Hendrix scrapers showing range in size.

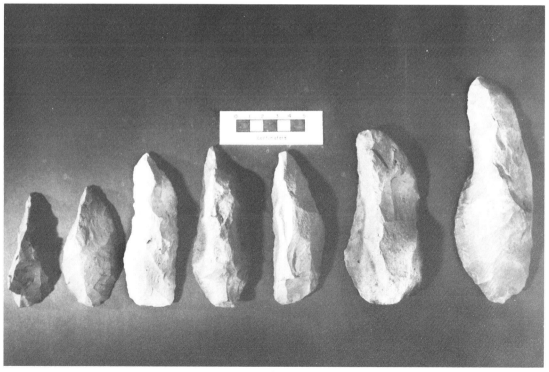

percussion and the angle of the used edges was steep (60–90 degrees). Eleven of the 33 specimens had striking platforms, two of which were at the tip as described by Witthoft. All members of the sample were considered unifacial but 14 exhibited a slight amount of flake removal to thin the bulb or the curvature of the ventral surface. Currently the author is conducting a more sophisticated study of these implements.

Snub-nosed scraper (oblong)

Specimens similar to that illustrated in figures 3*d* and 9 have been recovered at the Bull Brook (Wormington 1957:77), Eva (Lewis and Lewis 1961:55), and Reagan (Ritchie 1953:252) sites. In Florida, these implements, though not common, have been found at a number of locations. The illustrated example is from the CCA Site, Marion County. It weighs 40 g and is 7.0 cm long, 3.0 cm wide, and 1.5 cm thick. It resembles a miniature turtleback scraper of the Preceramic period, but the (length × width) ÷ (thickness ×100) index indicates that it is proportionately more slender than a

Figure 9. Snub-nosed scraper: *(a)* side view, *(b)* top view.

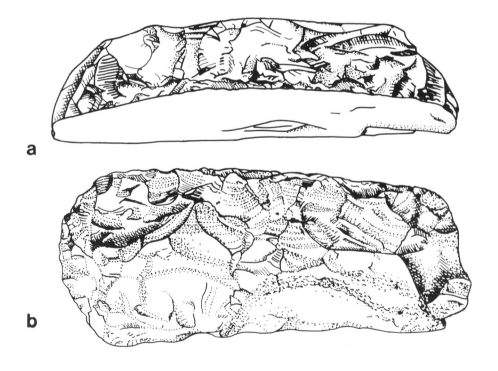

a

b

turtleback. It is difficult to determine whether the specimen was made from a thick blade or from a flake because the striking platform and bulb of force have been removed. The dorsal surface has multiple visible flake scars but the tool is so weathered that no original fracture features can be seen on the ventral surface. It has been percussion flaked to form an angle of 60 degrees, with an 80-degree angle resulting from use. The most intensive use occurred on both edges, as is evidenced by multiple scalariform step fractures. The bit may have served a different function than the edges or it may have been rejuvenated, thus obliterating previous evidence of use. The butt does not appear to have been used extensively, all evidence of use being on the dorsal surface. There is no indication that the specimen was hafted.

Implements similar to that illustrated in figure 3*f* are reported from the European Upper Paleolithic (Bordes 1968:156) and have been found in North America at Williamson (McCary 1951:14), Eva (Lewis and Lewis 1961:54), Shoop (Witthoft 1952), Stanfield-Worley (DeJarnette et al. 1962:86), Brand (Goodyear 1974:46), Hardaway (Coe 1964:75) and other sites in Arkansas (Morse 1973:36). I do not know of any report that describes Florida specimens of this type, but the type is represented in a number of collections. The specimen illustrated was recovered from the Santa Fe River, weighs 34 g, and is 4.5 cm long, 4.0 cm wide, and 1.7 cm thick. It has been percussion flaked to form an angle of 87 degrees at the distal end; the edge angles are 75–80 degrees. The tool appears to have been made from a thick truncated blade or flake. The dorsal surface has been extensively flaked. One flake has been removed from the ventral face to thin part of the bulb. The striking platform and a portion of the bulb remain. The specimen shows use on the distal end and on both sides. All evidence of use is on the dorsal surface and is indicated by multiple scalariform step fractures, with the edges showing evidence of the most intense use. It is possible that the bit was continually rejuvenated, thus removing former use scars. This procedure

Snub-nosed scraper (triangular)

21

might also account for the steeper edge angle of the bit. There is no indication that the specimen was hafted.

Carinate scrapers   Implements similar to that pictured in figure 3*e* are described by Bordes (1968:155–56) for the Upper Paleolithic and at Stanfield-Worley (DeJarnette et al. 1962:86), at Rose Island (Chapman 1975:137), at Russell Cave (Griffin 1974:49), and from Arkansas (Morse 1973:38). Cambron and Hulse (1973:7) call this an oval core scraper B-8. In Florida, carinate scrapers were recovered at the Nalcrest site (Bullen and Beilman 1973:18–19) and have been found elsewhere, e.g., in the Santa Fe River. The specimen in figure 3*e* weighs 23 g and is 3.3 cm in diameter and 1.3 cm thick, entirely unifacial, percussion flaked to form an angle of about 90 degrees, and appears to have been extensively used around its entire circumference. The striking platform and bulb are not present and there is no indication that the implement was hafted. These tools do not seem to have been common in the Paleo Indian period. Perhaps they should be assigned to the Late Paleo period although Cambron and Hulse (1973:7) report their recovery from sites that produced Paleo Indian artifacts.

Other artifacts   The specimens pictured in figure 3*g, h, k, q,* and *v* have been assigned to the Paleo Indian period because they share a number of attributes typical of early assemblages (i.e., they are unifacial blades or flakes and are pressure or percussion flaked to form a steep edge). At present, however, these objects cannot be "typed" based on the criteria defined on page 5. Similar artifacts are described for nearly all early sites in North America. Goggin (1950) illustrates comparable objects for Florida. Figure 3*g* and *v* were recovered from the Santa Fe River, *h* and *q* from the Johnson Lake site (Bullen and Dolan 1959), and figure 10*k* from the CCA Site about one mile from Johnson Lake in Marion County.

Further research will probably increase the number of artifacts assigned to the Paleo Indian period in Florida.

22

Figure 10. Stone tool kit of the Late Paleo period: (a) drill, (b) snub-nosed scraper (oblong), (c,d) snub-nosed scrapers (triangular), (e) unifacial scraper (ovoid), (f) miscellaneous scraper, (g) thumbnail scraper, (h) hafted end scraper made from broken point, (i) graver, (j) scraper with graver spur, (k) spokeshave with graver spurs, (l) bola stone, (m,n) Clear Fork gouge, (o,p,q) Edgefield scrapers, (r,s) blades, (t,u,v) Waller scraper-knives.

Stone Tool Typology

Late Paleo
period

Projectile points

The Bolen point (fig. 11) is present in quantity (see map 2, p. 62) and considerable variation exists within the type (Bullen 1975:51–52). Other projectile point types of the period have been recovered in Florida but are not common. The Greenbriar, Hardaway Side-Notched, and Nuckolls Dalton points are pictured in figure 11. Bullen (1975:44–53) describes these in detail.

Bolen points are side-notched and usually have basal grinding like the points of the Paleo Indian period. More than one-half of all Bolen points are opposite-beveled (see figs. 11 and 12), suggesting that they were resharpened while attached to the shaft. Brooks (1978:personal communication) believes that beveled Bolen points are primarily generalized cutting tools.

Sollberger (1971, 1978) has conducted an experimental study of edge-beveled knives. He hypothesized that the presence of beveling did not indicate a type of point originally manfactured with that characteristic. He dulled the knives by cutting leather, very soft woods, and other materials and tried various ways to resharpen the knives to make them last the longest possible time. An examination of artifacts shows very small microflaked bevel resharpening to be the initial resharpening stage. As Sollberger resharpened the knives beyond the microbevel stage, the beveling flakes had to be longer and longer as the edge backed into the thicker width of the knife. Six knives were bevel resharpened experimentally ten to twelve times on each of the four edges, a total of forty or more times per knife. In other experiments with bifacial resharpening, six or eight resharpenings finally made the knives so thin that the bodies were completely used up. The bevel resharpening made the knives last much longer than bifacial or unifacial resharpening (Sollberger 1978:16).

Workmanship in the production of the Bolen point often appears crude; it is sometimes thick in proportion to length and width. These points are generally not very large, usually measuring 3–5 cm but occasionally exceeding this length.

Whereas in Florida points from the Paleo period are usually recovered from rivers, Bolen points are found at land sites as well. When found in systematic excavations, they are often recovered

24

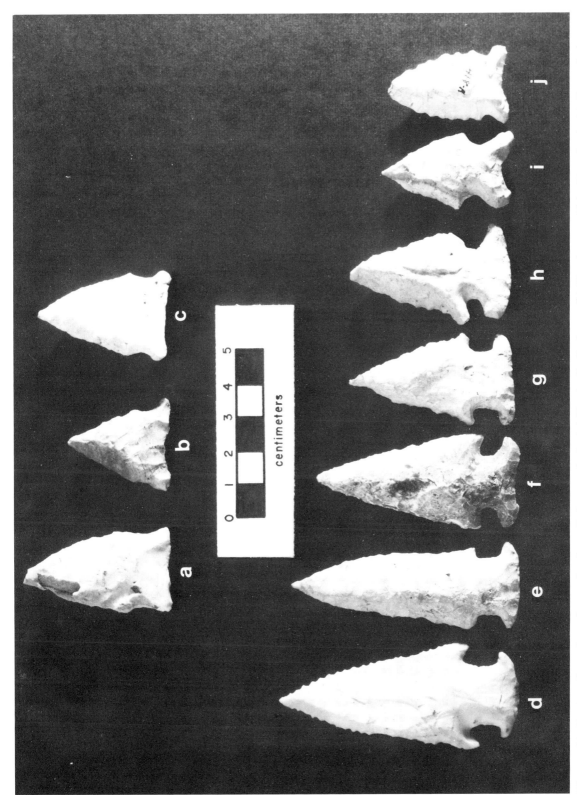

Figure 11. Projectile points from the Late Paleo period: (a) Nuckolls Dalton, (b) Hardaway Side-Notched, (c) Greenbriar, (d-j) Bolen point variants.

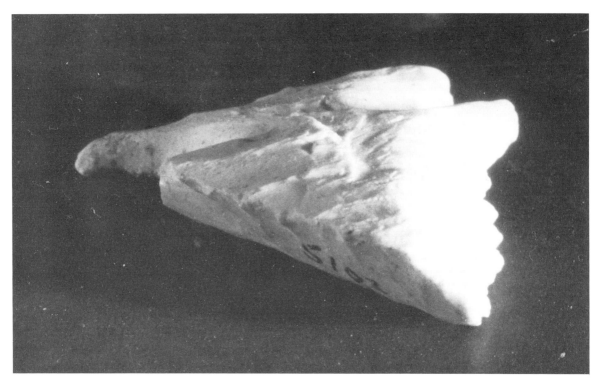

Figure 12. Opposite beveling seen on Bolen point.

with points of the Preceramic Archaic period. Since there is little stratigraphic documentation, the antiquity of the Bolen point is based on typological similarities to Late Paleo period points from sites outside of Florida that have been assigned fairly secure dates. Bolen points are found in far greater numbers in Florida than are Paleo Indian period points, suggesting a larger population during the Late Paleo period than during the previous period.

Edgefield scrapers

Specimens similar to that illustrated in figures 10*p, q*, and 13 are reported from Russell Cave (Griffin 1974:50), South Carolina, and elsewhere in the southeastern Gulf and southern Middle Atlantic states (Michie 1968, 1973). Warren (1973:119) describes this Florida tool type as a Piper-Fuller knife, "side-notched, unifacial, well made, beveled 'chisel' with a straight working edge or bit set at an angle of about 20 degrees to the long axis of the shank. Its skew blade calls to mind the Cody Knife of Wyoming, but there the resemblance ceases, for the latter is without side notches. In modern

26

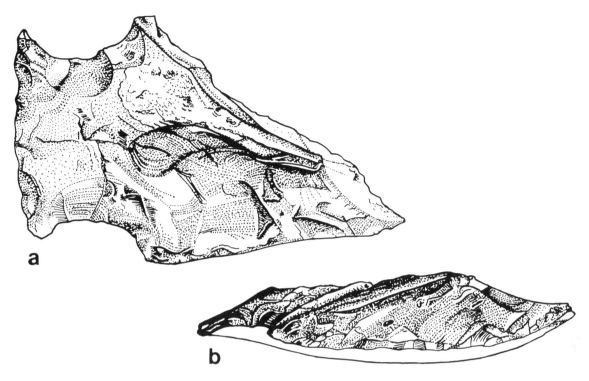

Figure 13. Edgefield scraper: *(a)* top view, *(b)* side view.

woodworking parlance it would be called a 'left skew chisel.'" The term *Edgefield scraper* will be used here to commemorate the original finds in Edgefield County, South Carolina, of a large number of implements of this type that Michie named after the area.

Michie (1973) conducted a detailed study of this tool, including techniques of manufacture and suggested its use based on an analysis of 21 specimens. Following Wilmsen's conclusions (1970), Michie believes the scraper was used to work bone because of the steep edge angle and the step fractures that extend over the dorsal face and sometimes into the ventral surface as well. "This suggests that the tool was drawn with heavy pressure over a tough unyielding surface somewhat in the fashion of an adze or plane" (Michie 1973:5).

The Edgefield scraper illustrated in figure 10*p* weighs 12 g and is 5.9 cm long, 3.0 cm wide, and .8 cm thick. It is unifacial except for the base and a slight amount of flaking on the ventral surface opposite the beveled edge. The base is ground. The dorsal surface has

27

been extensively flaked and the left edge has been pressure flaked to form a bevel with an angle of 70 degrees, probably from repeated resharpening. Tiny step fractures resulting from use have made the angle even steeper. The right edge may have been used as a knife.

The specimen pictured in figure 10*o* weighs 8 g and is 5.2 cm long, 2.8 cm wide, and .7 cm thick. It is unifacial except for the base and appears to have been made from a thinning flake or blade. The bulbar end is at the tip. The ventral face of the base has been finely pressure flaked and then ground. Both edges have been used as a scraper. The left edge has been pressure flaked to form a bevel with an angle of 60 degrees. Tiny step fractures resulting from use have made the angle even steeper. The tip and the right edge near the tip have received the most intensive use, perhaps as a chisel or gouge.

The specimen shown in figures 10*q* and 13*a, b* weighs 19 g and is 5.3 cm long, 3.3 cm wide, and 1.3 cm thick. It is unifacial except for the formation of the notches. The base is ground. The dorsal face has some secondary flaking but the cortex remains on the thickest portion. Steep flaking on the left edge forms a bevel with an angle of 85 degrees. Small step fractures on the beveled surface indicate the object was used as a scraper. More intense use or a different kind of use may have occurred near the tip. The right side of the specimen appears to have been used to rub something that eventually smoothed the edge.

Brooks (1978:personal communication) believes that since only the haft area is bifacial, the necessity for a haft with a minimum of irregularities is indicated. "From this, as well as the wide hafting area, I infer that a secure haft was emphasized for most efficiently carrying out heavy duty scraping and cutting functions on dense material such as bone. The wide haft would also be conducive to applying considerable pressure (force without breakage of the tool) at the haft, which would likely be an inherently weak spot."

Since Edgefield scrapers are side-notched like Bolen points, it is probably correct to assign them to the tool kit of the Late Paleo period. Statistical and ecological distribution studies of these implements are being conducted (Goodyear, Michie, and Purdy in preparation).

Implements similar to those illustrated in figure 10*m, n* have been described in a summary article by Hester et al. (1973), who state that these artifacts are triangular, bifacial or unifacial, with plano-convex cross sections and steeply beveled straight or convex working edges (although a small percentage have concave bits). The Hester group reports a considerable range in the dimensions of their sample of 54 specimens. The artifacts they studied must have a certain "look" about them because these are not very rigid criteria for establishing a type. The most common recurrent feature is the nibbling (small step fractures) on the dorsal face of the bit, which has an average angle of about 65 degrees. Hester et al. (1973:95) concluded that the Clear Fork gouge was not used in a gouging fashion but more in the manner of endscrapers to dress and smooth wood surfaces. These implements were probably hafted because many exhibit dulling and crushing of the lateral edges near the proximal end. The Dalton adze (Morse 1973:26) seems to be a comparable tool.

Clear Fork gouge

The specimen shown in figure 10*m* weighs 66 g and is 6.3 cm long, 4.4 cm wide, and 2.4 cm thick. It is bifacially flaked. The angle of the bit is about 62 degrees. Use fractures can be detected on both faces of the bit, indicating that it may have been used as a gouge.

Figure 10*n* weighs 40 g and is 5.5 cm long, 3.6 cm wide and 2.1 cm thick. It is bifacially flaked. The angle of the bit is about 67 degrees. Use wear is apparent in the step fracturing on the dorsal surface of the bit.

Clear Fork gouges are not known to be common in Florida, although they have a wide distribution in Texas and northeastern Mexico.

Specimens similar to that illustrated in figure 10*e* have been described for the Eva site (Lewis and Lewis 1961:55) and the

Unifacial scraper (ovoid)

Hardaway site (Coe 1964:78). The scraper shown in figure 10 weighs 43 g and is 4.9 cm long, 4.7 cm wide, and 1.5 cm thick, with the angle of the distal end 80 degrees. It is unifacial and the bulb of percussion is still present. The flake was detached from the core in a manner reminiscent of the Levallois technique and the edges of the artifact have been finely flaked to form a steep angle. Tiny step fractures are apparent on the dorsal surface of nearly the entire circumference. It is not known how common these specimens are in Florida.

Bola stones

Specimens similar to that illustrated in figure 10*l* are described by Simpson (1948), Neill (1971), and Waller (1969). Wormington (1957:138, 160) and Agogino (Mason 1962) mention grooved bolas as part of the Paleo Indian tool complex at some sites, but the Florida specimens are not grooved. Simpson says these objects are made of "sandstone, limestone, or quartz, are about the size and shape of a hen's egg, and have a shallow indentation in the smaller end" (1948:14). Although Simpson believes they were clubheads, they closely resemble specimens that are tied with thongs, knotted at the indentation, and thrown to ensnare the legs of running animals being hunted by South American Indians.

Figure 10*l* weighs 112 g and is 5.2 cm long, 4.2 cm wide, and 3.5 cm thick. It has been shaped, including the shallow indentation at one end, by a pecking and grinding technique. Since the original stone was probably a river-rounded cobble, it did not need to be altered greatly. The specimen shown is made from bog iron that could be native to Florida; however, many bolas are made of non-Florida stone.

Although it is not certain how common these implements are, I have seen more than one hundred examples, many recovered from the Santa Fe River. They are not found along with more recent material; therefore, they probably belong with either the Paleo Indian or Late Paleo tool kit, or both. While bola stones have not been identified widely through the southeast, Bullen (Neill 1971:70) says there have been surface finds as far north as Massachusetts.

I do not know if specimens similar to those illustrated in figure 10*t*, *u*, *v* have been found extensively outside of Florida. Waller (1971) describes these as unifacial, side-notched artifacts, the majority of which were recovered from the Santa Fe River in the vicinity of early "kill" sites. Bullen and Beilman (1973) discuss these as part of the stone tool assemblage at the Nalcrest site.

Waller hafted scraper-knife

Figure 10*t* weighs 10 g and is 5.3 cm long, 3.2 cm wide, and .7 cm thick. A thinning flake that has been modified by slight but uniform pressure flaking on one face of each side and by shaping the notches, this knife shows the result of flaking on the right dorsal and the left ventral face. Otherwise, the specimen is unifacial with the dorsal surface exhibiting multiple secondary flake scars typical of thinning flakes. The distal end and both edges were used as a scraper and possibly as a knife also because there are tiny hinge and step fractures on the faces opposite the pressure flakes. What appears to be scraper use may actually reflect resharpening of a dulled knife edge. The edge angle is about 50 degrees, the bulb of percussion and part of the ground striking platform are still present, and the notches were formed by removing flakes alternately from one face and then the other.

Figure 10*u* weighs 6 g and is 5.2 cm long, 1.4 cm wide, and .7 cm thick. This is a truncated blade formed by the microburin technique (Tixier 1974:17) with the notches formed by unidirectional flaking from the ventral to the dorsal surface. The specimen is unifacial and seems to have functioned as a knife because there are tiny use fractures on both faces of the edges. The truncated distal end may have been used as a burin. The bulb of percussion and the striking platform are missing. The edge angle is about 45 degrees.

Figure 10*v* weighs 12 g and is 6.1 cm long, 3.3 cm wide, and .6 cm thick. It was made from a thinning flake modified by very careful, uniform pressure flaking on one face of each edge and by forming the notches. The pressure flaking occurs on the dorsal surface of the right side and the ventral surface of the left side. The specimen is unifacial except for the pressure flaking. The dorsal surface has multiple secondary flake scars typical of thinning flakes, with the notches formed by flaking from the ventral to the dorsal surface only. The specimen appears to have functioned primarily as a scraper. The angle of the edge is about 52 degrees.

With regard to overall appearance, the most distinct morphological features of these implements are the side notches—the attribute that distinguishes them as a type (fig. 14). A more detailed analysis of Waller scraper-knives is being conducted (Purdy, in preparation).

Waller (1971) suspects that these artifacts may have been used to remove hides from animals and to slice portions of meat from carcasses. They are, as a whole, fragile tools, and the amount of wear they show does not suggest that they received very rough usage.

Other artifacts   Drills, various scrapers, and blades, already described for the Paleo Indian period, are also found through the Late Paleo period (fig. 10*a*−*k, r, s*). In fact, the stone tool assemblages of the two periods are difficult to distinguish. If there are any distinctions, the tools of the Late Paleo period are more diversified and may reflect a more settled population or more varied activities. The presence of the Clear Fork gouge in the Late Paleo tool kit is indicative of heavy woodworking activities such as canoe making and house construction.

Preceramic   Much of the information about the stone tools and their uses
Archaic period   described in this section was amassed by studying specimens from the Senator Edwards site (Purdy 1975*a*; Purdy and Beach 1980). Other sites in Florida yielding specimens used for comparison of Preceramic Archaic stone implements are the Newnan's Lake site (Clausen 1964), Johnson Lake site (Bullen and Dolan 1959), the Lake Kanapaha site (Hemmings and Kohler 1974), and Container Corporation of America site (Purdy 1981*a*).

Projectile points   Projectile points are typically large and stemmed, averaging 5−15 cm in length. It is generally agreed that those of this period were used with an atlatl, or spear-thrower. Figure 15*e, f,* and *g* illustrate early Preceramic Archaic points and 15*a, b, c,* and *d* are middle to

Figure 14. Waller scraper-knives.

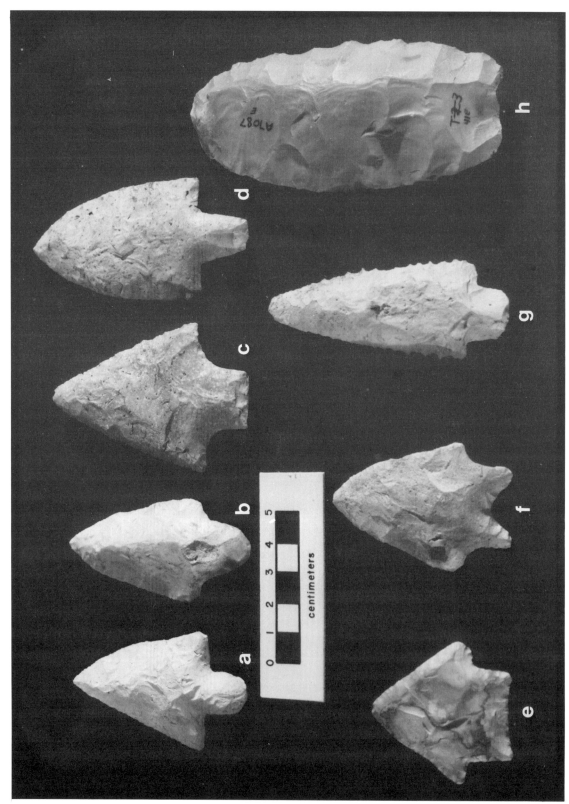

Figure 15. Projectile points of the Preceramic Archaic period: (a) Marion, (b) Putnam, (c) Levy, (d) Newnan, (e) Wacissa, (f) Arredondo, (g) Kirk serrated, (h) Preform.

late Preceramic Archaic points. See Bullen (1975: 30–43) for a description of these points and their chronological placement. Figure 15*h* shows a preform which might have been finished into any one of a number of Preceramic Archaic projectile point types. (See distribution map 3, p. 63.)

The specimens shown in figure 16*k, l* were recovered at the Senator Edwards site (Purdy 1975*a*), and similar examples have been found at a number of other locations in Florida.

Unifacial humpedback planes (turtleback scrapers)

Figure 16*k* weighs 261 g and is 11.1 cm long, 5.9 cm wide, and 4.0 cm thick. The original flake may have been obtained by a quartering or split cone technique (Crabtree 1972:92) because no evidence of a bulb of force, striking platform, or other fracture features remains on the ventral surface. The tool was shaped by removing flakes on the dorsal face to form an angle of about 55–60 degrees. Through use, the angle was steepened to 85 degrees at the bit, 78 degrees at the butt, and 80 degrees on the edges. The specimen is entirely unifacial but has four hinge fractures on the edges of the ventral surface that may have resulted accidentally from inappropriate use (Crabtree and Davis 1968). The dorsal surface shows multiple scalariform step and hinge fractures, most intense at the bit and on both edges near the bit (fig. 17). It does not appear to have been hafted.

Figure 16*l* weighs 702 g and is 14.9 cm long, 9.2 cm wide, and 5.5 cm thick. The ventral surface retains slight evidence that this implement was made from a flake detached from a large chert nodule because, even though the bulb and platform have been removed, the conchoidal nature of the fracture remains. A large amount of cortex is still present on the dorsal surface. The tool was shaped by removing flakes from the dorsal face to form an angle of about 55 degrees. Through use, the angle was steepened to 80 degrees at the bit, 65 degrees at the butt, and 75 degrees on the edges. The specimen is entirely unifacial but has three small hinge fractures on the edges of the ventral surface. The entire ventral surface shows polish, suggesting that the implement was held flat

35

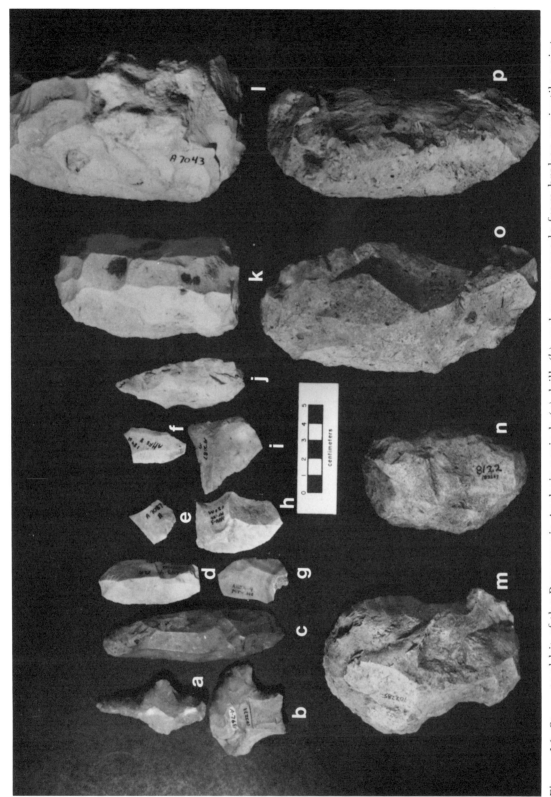

Figure 16. Stone tool kit of the Preceramic Archaic period: (*a*) drill, (*b*) end scraper made from broken projectile point, (*c,d*) blades, (*e,f,g*) truncated blades, (*h,i*) utilized flakes, (*j*) "knife," (*k,l,m*) unifacial humpedback planes, *m* is waisted, (*n,o,p*) miscellaneous scraping and chopping tools.

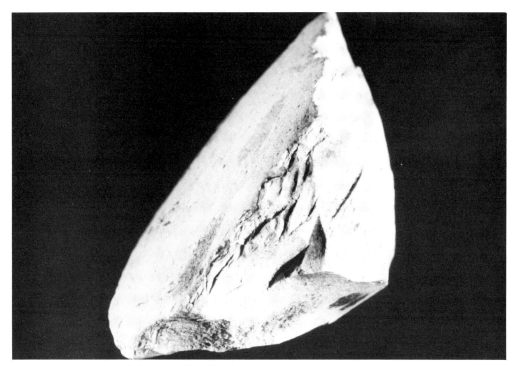

Figure 17. Unifacial humpedback plane.

and rubbed over a broad surface. Multiple scalariform step and
hinge fractures showing on the edges of the dorsal surface are most
intense at the bit and on both edges near the bit. It does not appear
to have been hafted.

Humpedback scrapers in an extreme range of sizes have been
found. These implements are suitable to work large or small pieces
of bone, wood, or hide. Humpedback scrapers have been placed in
the Preceramic Archaic period although there is not irrefutable
evidence that they are not associated with other periods. In
addition, the artifact assemblage from the Senator Edwards site was
primarily archaic although some Late Paleo points were present. My
impression is that they belong to the very early Preceramic Archaic
or the Late Paleo, being similar, in manufacture and in evident
use, to the much smaller unifacial oblong end scraper described
for the Paleo Indian and Late Paleo periods (figs. 3 and 10).
Although these tools could not have performed exactly the same

tasks because of the differences in their size, they may have been used on similar material (i.e., wood or bone).

Similar humpedback planes that are waisted, probably for hafting, are fairly common in Florida. Lewis and Lewis (1961:63) call this kind of implement an adze and consider it more recent than the unnotched adzes.

The scraper shown in figure 16*m* weighs 292 g and is 11.6 cm long, 7.6 cm wide, and 3.5 cm thick. The angle of the bit is 70 degrees. The bit and both edges near the bit have multiple scalariform step and hinge fractures on the dorsal face and the ventral surface is unifacial except in the hafting area.

Hemmings (1975:149) pictures a "notched adze" recovered at Silver Springs (Mr-92) and believes it dates to the Late Preceramic Archaic period 5000–4000 years ago. Bullen (1972:32) illustrates a similar specimen recovered from a zone containing early pottery at Site J-5 on the bank of the Chattahoochee River.

Other artifacts   Observations made at quarry workshop sites indicate that heavy utilization of Florida chert occurred during the early and middle Preceramic Archaic period. Paradoxically, except for a wide variety of projectile points (Bullen 1975; shown in fig. 15) and some stemmed end scrapers and drills (figs. 16*a, b*) made from projectile points, the greatest majority of the stone implements found at archaeological sites cannot be typed by the criteria defined at the beginning of this chapter. Blades (fig. 16*c*) were still in use during the Preceramic Archaic period but the classic form declined and truncated blades or bladelike flakes seem to have replaced spurred scrapers and graver spurs during the period. The truncated blades functioned as burins, scrapers, knives, or perforators. Utilized flakes have been recovered in all sizes, shapes, and types of use. They differ from utilized flakes of the earlier periods because they are unmodified; especially they do not have steep, uniform pressure retouch flaking. Other tools are bifacial and were used for cutting, scraping, chopping, pounding, gouging, etc. The tool kit of the Preceramic Archaic period displays a

38

tremendous diversity with regard to function, but the tools defy morphological classification.

The blade or bladelike flake in figure 16*d* weighs 14 g and is 6.0 cm long, 2.6 cm wide, and 1.0 cm thick. The implement has many characteristics of a blade including a central ridge, but the (length × width) ÷ (thickness × 100) index of .15 indicates a thicker specimen than a true blade that would be expected to have an average index of about .34. This tool has a prepared, ground striking platform and a diffuse bulb of force. It was used as a scraper along its left edge with most of the motion in use directed from the dorsal to the ventral surface, but a 1.5 cm area of the dorsal edge also was used as a scraper. The right side may have been used as a knife because very tiny fractures on both faces have removed the feathered edge. The angle of the used edge is about 50 degrees.

In figure 16*e* the truncated blade or bladelike flake appears to have been formed by the dihedral burin technique (Movius et al. 1968; Tixier 1974). The specimen has a small, prepared, ground platform. The tip could have been used effectively as a graver since close examination reveals tiny step fractures on the right side of the tip. It weighs 3 g and is 2.9 cm long, 2.6 cm wide, and .5 cm thick. Figure 16*f* shows the ventral surface of a truncated blade or bladelike flake. Evidence of scraping use shows along both edges and also near the tip on the dorsal surface; scraping use may have caused the specimen to break. A very pink area near the broken tip suggests that it was used for a heat-producing task. The striking platform is small and ground, and there is a small but noticeable bulb of force. The specimen weighs 3 g and is 3.9 cm long, 2.1 cm wide, and .4 cm thick. The angle of the used edge is about 50 degrees.

Figure 16*g* is a utilized thinning flake showing scraping use on the right side. The left side has been truncated, possibly through use because the specimen has become very fragile. The partially truncated tip has also been used as a scraper. It has a small, ground, prepared platform and a small but noticeable bulb of force. It weighs 5 g and is 4.2 cm long, 2.2 cm wide, and .4 cm thick. The angle of the used edge is about 45 degrees.

Figure 16*h* is a thick thinning flake that has been used as a scraper from the ventral to the dorsal surface at the distal end, as well as for scraping and possible cutting on the left side. It has a prepared, ground platform and a noticeable bulb of force. It weighs 17 g and is 5.3 cm long, 3.6 cm wide, and 1.3 cm thick. The angle of the distal end is 65–70 degrees.

Figure 16*i* is a thinning flake that has been utilized as a scraper, a cutting tool, and possibly as a perforator. The striking platform is ground, and the bulb of force is quite prominent (salient). It weighs 11 g and is 4.0 cm long, 4.0 cm wide, and .8 cm thick. The angle of the used distal end is about 60 degrees.

Truncated blades and utilized flakes generally are quite fragile and could not have been used to perform tasks demanding strength. They could have been used to cut, scrape, or pierce many materials, however, because the feathered edge of a freshly struck piece of chert is extremely sharp. Although they would have dulled rapidly, they were easily replaceable at the outcrop site with a similar tool. There is no evidence that figures 16*d*–*i* were hafted. At the Senator Edwards site (Purdy 1975*a*), 6,071 truncated blades and 4,602 utilized flakes were recovered from a trench 48 meters long and 1.5 meters wide. Measurements of a 10 percent random sample were made using the criteria in figure 18. Similar specimens were probably used during all time periods but cannot be placed chronologically if taken out of context.

Figure 16*j* is a small, thick, bifacial tool. It appears to have been used as a cutting or sawing tool especially on the right edge which has an angle of about 85 degrees. Alternatively it could be a novice's attempt to flintknap because the flaking is crude. It weighs 44 g and is 7.6 cm long, 3.1 cm wide, and 2.2 cm thick.

Figure 16*n* is bifacial and exhibits battering around the entire circumference. It is undoubtedly a hammerstone but may also have been used as a wedge. I see no indication that the specimen was hafted. It weighs 289 g and is 9.6 cm long, 6.3 cm wide, and 4.3 cm thick.

Although figure 16*o* is bifacial, it is possible to determine that the

Figure 18

Figure 18. Information recorded on data coding sheets

1-4   Artifact number (e.g., 0027)

5-6   Artifact category (e.g., 13=utilized flake)

7   Site (e.g., 2=CCA Site)

8   Area of find at site (0=surface; 1=backhoe trench; 2=trench two; 3=three-meter square)

9-10   Square (01=1; 02=2; 03=3; 04=4; 05=5; etc.)

11   Level (0=not dug by levels; 1=level one; 2=level two; etc.)

12   Type of site (1=workshop site; 2=quarry or outcrop; 3=habitation; 4=kill site; 5=mound; 6=quarry/workshop; etc.)

13   Area of site

14-16   Length in centimeters (e.g., 08.6)

18-20   Width in centimeters (e.g., 01.7)

22-23   Thickness in centimeters (e.g., 0.5)

25-27   Index [(length × width) ÷ (thickness × 100)]

29-33   Weight in grams (e.g., 0024.6)

35   Heated, leave blank if in question or not known (0=no; 1=yes; 2=used with heat; 3=exposed to heat or heat damaged)

37   Pressure flaked (e.g., 0=no; 1=slight; 2=yes)

39   Symmetry (e.g., 0=none; 1=poor; 2=fair; 3=good)

41   Signs of use, leave blank if undetermined (0=no; 1=yes, slight; 2=yes, heavy)

42-43   Type of use (00=abrader; 01=hammer; 02=scraper, etc.)

44   Patina (0=no; 1=slight; 2=moderate; 3=heavy; 4=chalky; 5=moderately patinated/reflaked; 6=heavily patinated/reflaked or shattered)

45   Solution weathering, rate is based on visual or subjective determination (0=no; 1=slight; 2=moderate)

46   Angle of use or angle of edge (O<50°; 1>50°, <75°; 2>75°)

49   Area of use (0=one area; 1=more than one area of use, single face; 2=more than one area of use, both faces)

52-54   Length of use, applicable mostly to scraping or cutting artifacts (e.g., 01.1)

56   Cortex (0=no; 1=yes)

57   Flake type (0=primary flake with cortex; 1=secondary flake with little or no cortex but also no multiple flake scars; 2=secondary flake with scarson dorsal surface; 3=flake with bifacial flaking)

58   Novice craftsman, subjective determination used only for projectiles (0=no; 1=yes)

61   Striking platform, leave blank if missing (0=big; 1=small; 2=prepared/big; 3=prepared/small; 4=ground or roughed up/big; 5=ground or roughed up/small)

63   Bulb of force (1=salient; 2=diffuse)

65   Type of projectile point (1=Paleo; 2=Bolen; 3=Archaic; 4=Early Ceramic; 5=Late Ceramic; 6=other or undetermined)

66   Type of Archaic

68   For blades only (1=triangular; 2=trapesoid; 3=triangular/nibbled; 4=trapesoid/nibbled; 5=nibbled)

specimen is a large flake that must have been struck from the core with tremendous force because it almost terminated in a hinge fracture visible on the ventral surface. The implement was used as a scraper on the ventral face of the left edge and the dorsal face of the right edge toward the distal end. The angle of use is 85 degrees. Other areas on the specimen could have been used for scraping or cutting but this could not be determined by examination. Flake removal is not uniform either in size or direction. I see no indication that the specimen was hafted. It weighs 463 g and is 10.3 cm long, 7.4 cm wide, and 4.0 cm thick.

Although figure 16*p* has had flakes removed from the ventral surface, the implement is primarily unifacial. Extreme battering or crushing on both edges and on the dorsal ridge suggests that it was used as a chopper. There are also multiple scalariform step fractures at the bit that might have resulted from adzing or gouging. Again I see no indication that the specimen was hafted. It weighs 599 g and is 15.7 cm long, 7.0 cm wide, and 5.0 cm thick.

At the Senator Edwards site about 2,500 large unifacial and bifacial implements have been recovered. Of these, only the turtleback scrapers can be "typed" by the criteria mentioned on page 5. After numerous attributes were recorded for all specimens, it was concluded that there is no uniformity in size, shape, function, or location of use on the implements. It was further concluded that the final shape of most of these implements resulted from (1) the use to which they were subjected, (2) the length of time they were used, (3) the later removal of flakes to rejuvenate an edge, or (4) the removal of flakes to be utilized for other purposes, i.e., the parent rock may not have been used at all (fig. 19*a*, *b*). Most of the implements exhibit multipurpose use. Evidence of scraping, chopping, cutting, pounding, and even piercing often can be detected on a single artifact (Purdy 1975*a*:183). Hemmings and Kohler (1974:62) reach a similar conclusion after studying Preceramic Archaic period stone remains from the Lake Kanapaha, Johnson Lake, Dixie Lime Cave, Silver Springs, and Bolen Bluff sites of Florida.

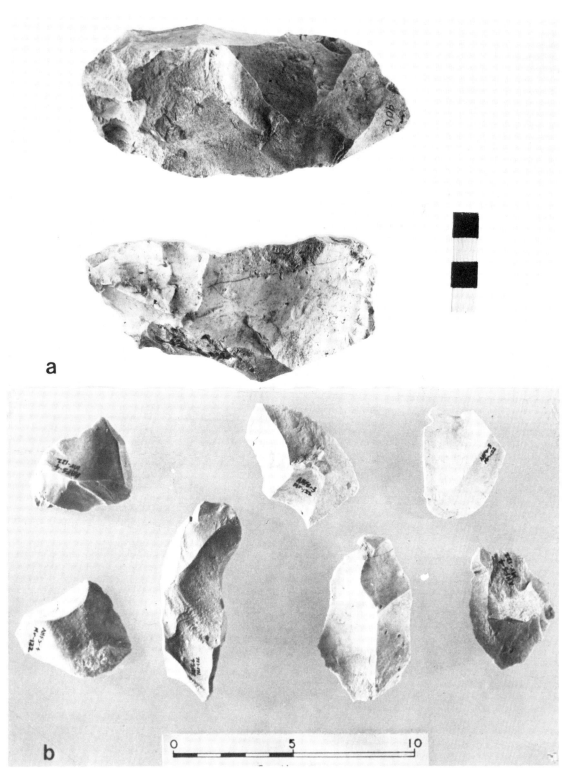

Figure 19. Cores and flakes: *(a)* cores with flake scars, scale in cm, *(b)* flakes similar to those removed from the cores that could be used effectively without further modification.

Stone Tool Typology

Many of the large stone tools of the Preceramic Archaic period in Florida resemble those described in various publications for the Southeast that have been classified into types and subtypes (e.g., Broyles 1971:40). Such a breakdown in classification for the Florida material may be possible if subclasses are defined (Purdy and Beach 1980).

Early Ceramic period

Projectile points

Bullen has demonstrated that a number of stemmed projectile points typical of the latter part of the Preceramic Archaic period were still used after the introduction of pottery although they tended to be smaller and not as well made (Bullen 1955, 1969, 1972). Just prior to the introduction of pottery and continuing through Orange and Florida Transitional times, nicely made basal and corner-notched points appeared (Bullen 1975:3, 24–28) (distribution map 4, p. 64). These include Culbreath, Clay, Lafayette, Citrus, and Hernando types (fig. 20).

Figure 20. Projectile points of the Early Ceramic period: *(a)* Culbreath, *(b)* Clay, *(c)* Lafayette, *(d)* Citrus, and *(e)* Hernando.

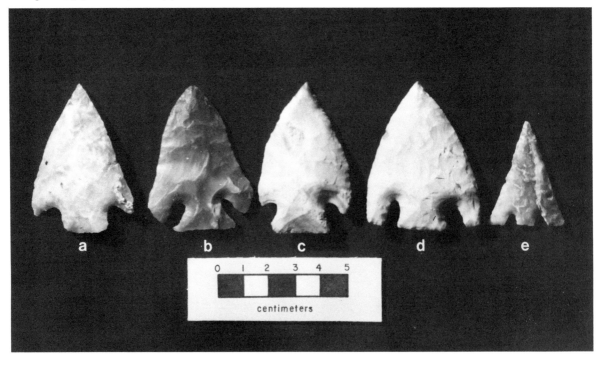

Early Ceramic microliths

Assemblages of microcores, blades, and tools similar to the 3,000-year-old Jaketown microlith industry of Louisiana appeared during the Early Ceramic period. Tool characteristics observed at these excavations suggest Early Ceramic period influences along the Gulf Coast from Louisiana to Florida (Lazarus 1958; Fairbanks 1959; Bullen and Bullen 1974; Haisten 1974; Reichelt 1974; Watson 1974). Morse and Tesar (1974) compare microliths from the Palm Court site in Bay County, Florida, and date them with those of the Cahokia microlith industry of the Early Mississippi period (A.D. 700). Knight (1976) describes the technology involved in manufacturing microliths found at Maximo Point in St. Petersburg and concludes that it differs significantly from that of the Jaketown specimens. Although the distribution of the microlith industry in Florida is restricted primarily to the Gulf Coast, Hemmings (1975) reports the recovery of microtools from a Preceramic Archaic zone at Silver Springs, Florida. With more careful inspection of collected stone remains, it is likely that a broader distribution will be recognized. It is known that prehistoric Florida peoples used microliths as scrapers, drills, knives, perforators, and gravers.

Microliths

Figure 21*c, d, e* illustrate microliths from Bay County, Florida. The microcore weighs 22 g and is 5.6 cm long; the blade weighs 3 g and is 3.6 cm long, 1.6 cm wide, and .8 cm thick. It was utilized as a knife as well as a scraper on both edges and the bit. The angle of the edges is about 65 degrees, the bit angle is 55 degrees. The microtool weighs less than 1 g and is 2.5 cm long, .9 cm wide, and .6 cm thick. It is completely unifacial and has been used as a scraper and possibly as a perforator. The edge angles are about 70 degrees.

Hafted end scrapers and drills continued to be made from projectile points (figs. 21*a, b*).

Other artifacts

During this period pendants, gorgets, plummets, celts, axes, hoes, and other objects made of steatite, igneous rock, mica, copper, other non-Florida material, and shell appeared and apparently increased until European contact in the 1500s (fig. 22).

Although little attention has been directed toward the chipped

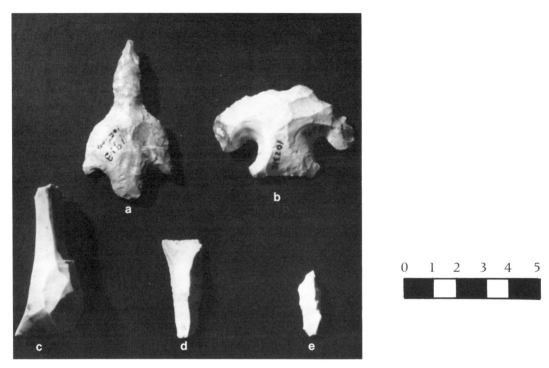

Figure 21. Microtools and other stone implements of the Early Ceramic Period: *(a)* drill, *(b)* hafted end scraper, *(c)* microcore, *(d)* microblade, *(e)* microtool.

Figure 22. Shell implements and tools made of non-Florida stone.

stone implements where ceramic artifacts have been discovered, it
has been observed that, other than microliths, the implements seem
to differ little from those of preceding periods. There is evidence that
a number of chert outcrop workshop sites in the central highlands of
Florida, heavily exploited during the Preceramic Archaic period, were
rarely utilized during the Early Ceramic period. These include the
Kanapaha site in Alachua County and the CCA and Senator Edwards
sites in Marion County. A great deal of research is still needed
concerning the question of probable declining use of these stone
resources. In the meantime my general impression is that
stoneworking technology declined drastically during this period.

A notable exception to my supposition is the Johns Island site in
Hernando County (Bullen and Bullen 1950) where large, nicely
made unifacial and bifacial chert implements, evidently made
during the Early Ceramic period, have been recovered. Examination
of these specimens suggests they were used as adzes, choppers,
wedges, etc. They are similar in form and function to artifacts
already described from the Preceramic Archaic period except that
more care was taken in their production.

Many points from this period are small, perhaps signaling the
appearance of the bow and arrow, but the continued uncovering of
larger points indicates that the spear was not entirely replaced.
Workmanship is usually crude and reinforces the conclusion that
stoneworking had declined and was not considered a prestigious
occupation. Chipping often does not cross the face of the point.
Sometimes the points are merely shaped flakes with some pressure
retouch on the edges. Some of the projectiles appear to be reworked
archaic forms. Points of this period are illustrated and described by
Bullen (1975:8–23). Pinellas, Duval, Columbia, and Jackson points
are shown in figure 23. Pinellas points, considered by Bullen to be
the most recent, have been recovered by the thousands.

Late Ceramic period

Projectile points

Chipped stone tools recovered at sites of this period tend to be
rather nondescript. They sometimes resemble crude Preceramic

Other artifacts

47

Figure 23. Projectile points of the Late Ceramic period: *(a)* Columbia, *(b)* Jackson, *(c)* Duval, *(d)* Pinellas, *(e)* drill probably made from a Pinellas point.

Archaic specimens and are probably reworked archaic forms. The evidence for this is manifest in three ways: (1) reflaking, after a long lapse of time, is apparent in differential patina on many specimens (fig. 24); (2) in spite of the fact that Florida has very few sites with stratigraphic sequences, the most nicely flaked stone implements recovered in situ are found in preceramic or earlier contexts; and (3) very few points or ceramics of the Late Ceramic period are found at the workshop sites in the central highlands. However, additional problems of identification remain because much of the physical evidence of recent Florida prehistory has come from mounds where artifacts from many time periods have been found, often mixed with mound fill.

An increasing number of implements made of shell and non-Florida stone materials were manufactured during the Late Ceramic period and there are rare finds of Hopewellian-like ceremonial blades.

48

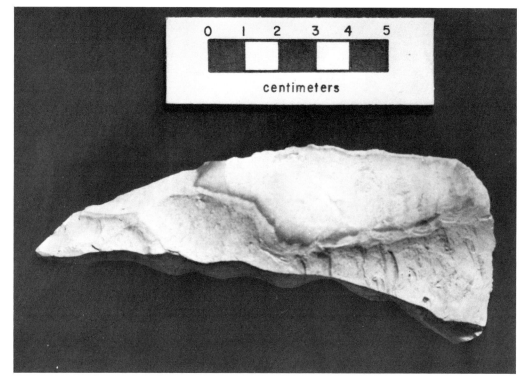

Figure 24. Patinated and restruck artifact (note the light area where a flake was removed after considerable weathering had occurred).

The earliest human tool may have been a stone hammer, an implement undoubtedly used during all of Florida's prehistory. In most areas of the world, river-rounded cobbles are abundantly available and have long been used as pounding instruments. In Florida, since only a few rivers provided cobbles, the Indians used chert to make their hammers. Anyone who has ever tried to "round off" a piece of chert knows it is not easy to create an angle greater than 90 degrees; therefore it is safe to say that hammers gained in value as they became more rounded through use. Most recovered hammerstones have extremely crushed surfaces resulting from longtime use. Occasionally, hammerstones are found that have failed after long, hard service. The hammerstone in figure 25 weighs 195 g and is 5.3 cm in diameter and 4.6 cm thick.

The dorsal surfaces of the objects pictured in figure 26 are crushed as a result of some material being laid on the anvil and hit with

Stone implements from undetermined periods

Hammerstones

Anvils

49

Figure 25. Hammerstone (note the crushing on the surface).

Figure 26. Anvils (note the crushing on the surface).

another stone. Any number of different kinds of tasks could have been accomplished with such an arrangement. Most of the anvils I have seen exhibit multipurpose use. The specimen shown in figure 26*b* has failed from long, hard wear. The cleaved surface is not the expected smooth, conchoidal fracture of chert but instead exhibits an uneven appearance. It weighs 1,855 g and is 15.5 cm long, 12.9 cm wide, and 9.2 cm thick. Figure 26*a* weighs 1,665 g and is 18.7 cm long, 14.0 cm wide, and 6.5 cm thick. It is completely unifacial, the ventral surface is polished, and the entire periphery was used for heavy scraping. This implement is very similar to the scraper-plane pictured in figure 16*l*. The striking platform still present in 25*a* is small and prepared, an unusual feature on such a large specimen. Similar implements are probably more common than presently apparent since anvils are not the kind of tool that attracts the amateur collector. In addition, their large size and unnotable shape make them easier to overlook than projectile points.

Abraders

Occasionally, abrading wear is observed on materials such as sandstone, pottery sherds, etc. I have rarely seen evidence of abrading use on chert except for striations on the cortex of some specimens.

Grindstones

Implements used as metates are present in Florida though not abundantly. In the 1500s one observer mentioned that the Indians "pound on a stone the aromatics that are to be used for seasoning" (Bennett 1968).

Discussion

Several questions arise from studying the lithic assemblages of the prehistoric time periods of Florida. It is fairly certain that the tool kits changed from unifacial tools made on blades in the Paleo Indian and Late Paleo periods to bifacial tools made on flakes in the Preceramic Archaic period. By the middle Preceramic Archaic, chipped stone technology had begun to decline as shown by less precise stoneworking techniques. Why these changes occurred may never be understood fully. The fact that many of the implements of the Paleo

Indian and Late Paleo periods resemble Old World Upper Paleolithic types suggests that a steady state had been reached in stone tool technology. It could also mean that thousands of years passed before the people were stimulated by a diffusion of ideas to change their tool-making techniques.

The stone tool kit of the Paleo period consists of task-specific implements such as thumbnail, oblong, and Hendrix scrapers, specialized tools which were carried over into the Late Paleo period. Other cultural changes undoubtedly were taking place during the Late Paleo period, but Florida Indians did not change their types of stone implements except for an increase in the number of projectiles and except for the addition of the Clear Fork gouge that suggests the presence of a larger and more stable population having woodworking skills. It is inconceivable that the Paleo Indians did not use wood, but I think it is likely that these nomadic peoples were not felling trees for building houses or making canoes. This probability is indicated by their kit of small lightweight tools and by the absence of any large woodworking tools.

At any rate, as Byers (1962:249) has pointed out, "anyone who has ever handled [Paleo Indian] material will recognize it at once." With the arrival of the Preceramic Archaic period we observe what appears to be an abrupt and drastic change in stone tool tradition. There is a noticeable change in tools that suggest a sedentary rather than migratory population.

One could speculate that the Paleo Indian and Late Paleo peoples performed a narrower range of tasks, while the more diversified and complex life of Preceramic Archaic peoples demanded an efficient but less elaborate stoneworking technology. Since the large quarries were near the settlements in north-central Florida, it was not necessary for people first to work stone into tools and then to carry them elsewhere to use them. Instead they could bring other materials that would be worked into finished tools (bone, hide, etc.) to their quarry sites, as Bryan (1950) suggests. Since the stone was serving the Preceramic Archaic implement maker only as a tool to make a tool, it is not surprising that little care was taken in shaping it. Carefully finished projectile points are, of course, an exception to this practice, and it is interesting to observe that the only continuity seen in the Preceramic Archaic stone tool industry is in the manufacture of points.

Characteristically, projectile point styles change through time, reflecting the changes in hafting, the switch from a thrusting spear to an atlatl, the introduction of the bow and arrow, and the dynamism in all parts of the culture (fig. 27). It might be revealing to make a thorough investigation of the basal and corner-notched projectile points, which represent a quite radical difference in manufacture from that of stemmed points. Their introduction suggests an intrusion of people or ideas since they occur along with rather than replace the stemmed points. In addition, the specimens I have examined seem to be made of a finer-grained stone material than most of the stemmed varieties—an observation that may indicate a limited procurement area.

Figure 27. Comparison of Florida projectile points of different time periods: *(a)* Paleo Indian, *(b)* Late Paleo Indian, *(c)* early Preceramic Archaic, *(d)* middle Preceramic Archaic, *(e)* Early Ceramic, *(f)* Late Ceramic.

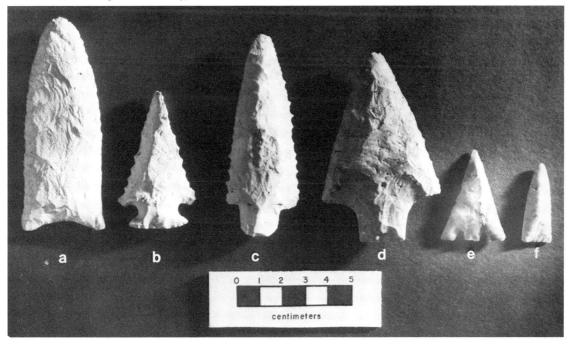

Stone Tool Typology

I have difficulty in determining whether many implements other than points had been hafted. Ethnographic accounts, historic records, and experimentation indicate that hafting is advantageous because it provides greater mechanical force. Some Florida implements may have had a socketed haft, which should not require as much smoothing of the tools' stone edges, usually necessary to prevent severing the binding material.

A series of little-noted changes throughout the Preceramic Archaic period resulted in a decline in stoneworking technology that appears in the archaeological record of the Early Ceramic period as a rapid, drastic decline (Renfrew 1978:203).

At first glance, one might conclude that implements from the Preceramic Archaic period represent the zenith of stoneworking technology. Florida Indians' most intense exploitation of chert sources occurred during this time and they produced large numbers of stone implements. But quantity is not quality. Most of the task-specific stone tools of the earlier periods were replaced by multipurpose implements that defy classification because no consistent progression of steps in manufacture was followed. Flakes struck from cores were used unmodified in numerous ways—a fact true also of nearly all of the large stone implements of the Preceramic Archaic period. This discontinuity probably could have been predicted because it appears that (1) there was a shift in economic base away from primary emphasis on hunting to greater dependence on marine and freshwater resources; (2) regionalism developed and settlements were in areas where there were no chert outcrops; and (3) industries developed other than stone-working ones, utilizing raw materials that were capable of accomplishing the necessary tasks, easier to obtain, and easier to work.

Stone tool utilization

It is not possible to identify the specific tasks performed with the stone tools of Florida, but a study of wear patterns and edge angles on stone objects recovered from prehistoric sites may result in a determination of tool function. I have examined thousands of objects with the aid of a 5× hand lens. If magnification is much greater than

54

$5\times$, features that naturally accompany chert fracture can be confused with evidence of use. There are times, of course, when it is advantageous to use a microscope.

In Florida, no experiments have been conducted to reproduce wear patterns on chert tools using materials available to the early inhabitants. Futhermore, historic records do not describe the Indians' use of stone. Ethnographic accounts from other geographic areas, particularly by Gould et al. (1971) and White (1967), and the results of experimentation conducted by other investigators provide worthwhile information but should be used with caution (see, for example, Ackerly 1978).

It is important to remember that chert implements cannot be used in all the same ways as metal. One kind of chert implement we should not expect to find would be, for example, twisting tools, except drills, because chert cannot withstand the stress of a twisting motion. If twisting tools were needed, bone or certain hard woods would have been more satisfactory.

Much like metal tools, chert implements can be used for a long time to scrape, adze, plane, and gouge, and their usefulness can be extended by resharpening the edge. Lithic remains provide abundant and easily recognizable indications of such functions. On the other hand, chert implements may not always carry evidence of the cutting use they have received. Cutting implements used as choppers should be fairly large and exhibit extreme crushing on the edges. A cutting tool used for sawing would leave small hinge or step fractures on both faces near the edge. A blade or flake used for slicing, however, might not have continued to be usable if it became clogged with flesh and would thus have been discarded before it dulled. It probably would have been too fragile to resharpen. When such stone implements are examined by the archaeologist thousands of years later, no evidence of cutting use will be found.

Piercing and graving implements are often difficult to recognize. Edges suitable for piercing and graving can occur accidentally— a blade that collapses when it is being detached because it is too thin, a flake that "steps off," debitage that is stepped on and snapped.

When no repetitive form specimens are found, confirmation of the piercing and incising function is tenuous.

Drills may be misnamed; close examination of the edges and tips of a number of drills in the Florida State Museum collections reveals very little evidence of rotary use. Nor is there much evidence to indicate that drills used as hafted knives were repeatedly resharpened as Witthoft suggests (1968:13). They may, however, be novices' attempts at pressure flaking. These drills resemble my first efforts to remove flakes by pressure when, since I could not cross the midline to thin, the outer dimensions became smaller and smaller while the thickness of the cross section remained the same—exactly like a drill.

Many of the stone remains I have examined were used with heat or generated enough heat during use to change color, indicative of thermal alteration. Since only a section of the implements had been affected by heat, it is possible to conclude that they were not intentionally thermally altered (Purdy and Brooks 1971). The implements were used as scrapers and perforators. Although there are ethnographic accounts describing stone tools used with fire to accomplish tasks like shaping fire-hardened sticks, hollowing out logs for canoes, and piercing holes in hides, there are no accounts describing the effect of heat on the stone tools themselves.

The color of the specimen illustrated in figure 28 is between very pale orange and pale yellowish brown (10 YR 6.5/2) except for the tip, which is between pale reddish brown and dark reddish brown (10 R 4/4) (Munsell 1946). The stone must have been subjected to temperatures of at least 250°C for this color change to occur. Some of the specimens exhibit the vitreous luster indicative of thermal alteration requiring a temperature of 350°C.

General problems arise when dealing with interpretation of lithic remains. Few systematic excavations or analyses of stone implements have been conducted (Purdy 1975a). Most of the types available for study come from private collections, and there has been only selective recovery of objects recognizable as stone tools, principally projectile points. This of course means incomplete sampling from

56

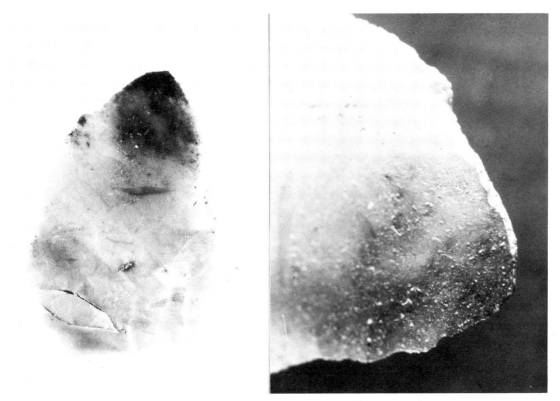

Figure 28. Flake used with heat (note the darker color in the area of use).

recovery sites since debitage and large or less exciting implements have been left behind or discarded. Stone tools recovered from sites other than workshop areas, such as villages, will look different because they tend to have been used more intensively for a longer time and have been resharpened. Therefore, they are difficult to compare with remains at quarries even if they served the same purpose. This produces a quandry for the researcher in that the greatest number of artifacts are available at quarries, while the greatest evidence of an artifact's use and wear is found at other sites.

One method of approaching the problem of interpretation is to correlate the pounding, scraping, cutting, and piercing functions of stone tools with the raw materials available to the early inhabitants of Florida and to suggest the stone tool type that might have been employed to accomplish a task. Table 2 is a simplistic attempt at such a reconstruction.

Table 2
Proposed uses of stone implements

Material worked	Stone function				Edge angle		Stone tool type			Evidence of use
	Pound	Scrape	Cut	Pierce	Low (<55°)	Steep (>55°)	Paleo period	Dalton period	Archaic period	
Wood										
Treefelling			▲			▲			Chopper	Pronounced
Houses		▲	▲			▲		Clear fork gouge	Plane, Adze, Saw	Pronounced
Posts	▲	▲	▲			▲	Hendrix scraper	Clear fork gouge	Chopper, Adze, Hammer	Pronounced
Canoes	▲	▲			▲	▲		Clear fork gouge	Wedge, Adze	Pronounced
Art objects		▲	▲	▲	▲	▲	Thumbnail scraper, Drill, End scraper, Blade, Spurred scraper, Snub-nosed scraper, Carinate scraper, Graver		Utilized flake, Blade, Truncated blade, Drill, End scraper	Pronounced Slight
Spear shafts		▲	▲		▲	▲	Thumbnail scraper, Blade, Hafted spokeshave, Carinate scraper, Snub-nosed scraper, End scraper, Spurred scraper		End scraper, Utilized flake, Blade	Pronounced
Furniture		▲	▲	▲	▲	▲	Hendrix scraper, End scraper, Drill, Snub-nosed scraper, Graver, Carinate scraper, Blade	Clear fork gouge	Adze, Saw, Knife, Blade, Scraper, Utilized flake, Drill, End scraper	Pronounced
Bone										
Handles		▲	▲			▲	Hendrix scraper, Thumbnail scraper, Blade, Snub-nosed scraper, Carinate scraper, End scraper, Spurred scraper, Hafted spokeshave	Beveled bolen, Edgefield scraper	Adze, Saw, Knife, Blade, Scraper, Utilized flake, Drill, End scraper	Pronounced
Points		▲	▲			▲	Hendrix scraper, Thumbnail scraper, End scraper, Blade, Snub-nosed scraper, Knife, Carinate scraper	Beveled bolen, Edgefield scraper	Adze, Saw, Knife, Blade, Scraper, Utilized flake, End scraper	
Art objects		▲	▲	▲	▲	▲	Thumbnail scraper, Drill, End scraper, Graver, Spurred scraper, Carinate scraper, Snub-nosed scraper, Blade, Beveled bolen, Edgefield scraper		Utilized flake, Blade, Truncated blade, Drill, End scraper	Pronounced Slight
Animals										
Hide		▲	▲	▲	▲		Snub-nosed scraper, Carinate scraper, End scraper, Ovoid scraper, Drill, Unifacial flake, Spurred scraper		Utilized flake, Drill, Scraper, Truncated blade, Unifacial scraper	Slight (Polish)
Bone	▲		▲			▲	Hammer, Blade, Graver		Hammer, Chopper, Blade, Truncated blade	Pronounced
Flesh			▲			▲	Blade, Waller knife, Waller scraper		Blade, Utilized flake	Slight
Plants										
Food	▲		▲			▲	Blade, Hammer, Anvil		Hammer, Anvil, Blade, Utilized flake	Pronounced Slight
Fiber (e.g., Cane, basketry)	▲	▲	▲			▲	Hammer, Blade, Anvil, Thumbnail scraper, End scraper		Hammer, Blade, Anvil, End scraper, Utilized flake, Knife	Pronounced Slight Polish
Feathers		▲	▲			▲	Blade		Blade, Utilized flake	Slight
Scarification			▲	▲		▲	Blade, Graver		Blade, Utilized flake, Truncated blade	Slight
Stone (e.g., Shaping projectile points)	▲						Hammer, Anvil		Hammer, Anvil	Pronounced

Distribution of projectile points

Map 1, showing the distribution of Paleo Indian projectile points, is modified from a map compiled by Mr. Ben I. Waller of Silver Springs, Florida (see also Waller 1969, 1970; Waller and Dunbar 1977). Information about single finds is not available. Maps 2–5 were compiled from the Florida State Museum collections and from the collection of Mr. Alvin Hendrix of McIntosh, Florida. It should be pointed out that these five maps are not intended to represent absolute numbers of projectile points found in Florida. The artifacts are so scattered among thousands of individuals that it would be futile to attempt a comprehensive catalog. The Hendrix collection is primarily from the Suwannee, Santa Fe, Waccasassa, and Oklawaha rivers. Other rivers, such as the Chipola and Aucilla, therefore, are not adequately represented but points from all time periods have been found in them. The Florida State Museum has artifacts from all counties in the state but primarily from the more extensively investigated areas (e.g., Alachua County). Even lacking complete series of specimens, however, a number of tentative observations can be made after comparing the geographic distribution and relative densities of points from the major time periods.

Very few Paleo Indian spearheads are found in the Suwannee River or the St. Marys River compared to the number found in other rivers and compared to points of more recent time periods found in the Suwannee.

Both the Suwannee and the St. Marys originate from the Okefenokee Swamp. The paucity of Paleo Indian artifacts from the Suwannee and the St. Marys may indicate that these rivers were without water at the end of the Pleistocene (12,000–10,000 years ago), a very important possibility that needs to be investigated. Paleo Indian points have been found east of the St. Johns River but they are not plentiful. The distribution of Paleo points indicates a population following the rivers and resources of the Florida Highlands and along the Gulf Coast. There may be many submerged sites along the coast that were drowned by the rising sea level. Waller (1978:personal communication) estimates that about 1.5 percent of artifacts recovered from Florida rivers are Paleo Indian

Distribution of projectile points in Florida

59

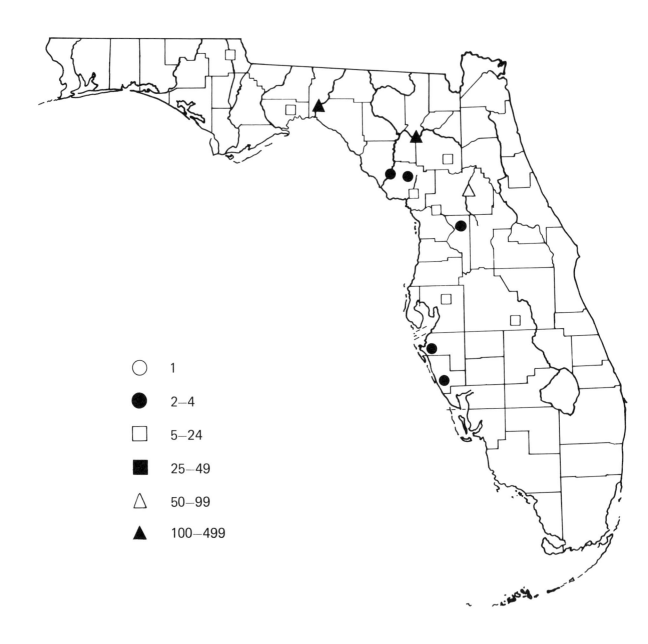

Map 1. Distribution of projectile points from the Paleo Indian period.

with about 5 percent recovered from the Santa Fe River being Paleo Indian.

If the single find locations east of the St. Johns were removed from map 2, the distribution of projectile points during the Late Paleo period would be similar to that of the Paleo Indian period with three important differences: (1) hundreds of Bolen points from the Late Paleo period are found in the Suwannee whereas Paleo Indian points are scarce; (2) there is a tremendous increase in numbers of Late Paleo period projectiles over Paleo Indian, especially significant in view of the shorter duration of the Late Paleo period; and (3) many of the Late Paleo period points are found at land as well as river sites whereas nearly all of the Paleo points are from rivers.

The long Preceramic Archaic period accounts for many thousands of stemmed projectile points. Map 3 indicates that this period reflects a wider distribution than the previous two periods. Florida's climate may have been wet and warm throughout most of this long time span. It is possible to distinguish three separate eras: an early Preceramic Archaic with points such as Kirk serrated, Wacissa, and Arredondo; a middle Preceramic Archaic with points such as Newnan, Putnam, Levy, and Marion (Bullen 1975:30–43); and the less easily identifiable late Preceramic Archaic, difficult to separate from the Early Ceramic period. There is, in fact, evidence that similar point types were made after the introduction of pottery but the points tend to become smaller and less well made (Bullen 1975:3).

Map 4 is a special map showing only the distribution of basally notched or corner-notched points such as Citrus, Clay, and Hernando. These points are stylistically quite different from the stemmed points of the Preceramic Archaic period, probably continued into the Early Ceramic period. The distribution suggests a population living primarily along the Gulf Coast and in the central highlands. A small number of these points have been recovered. It should be noted that the area where the greatest concentration of these points occurs is not the area where the earliest pottery has been reported in Florida.

Map 5 shows the distribution of points produced during more

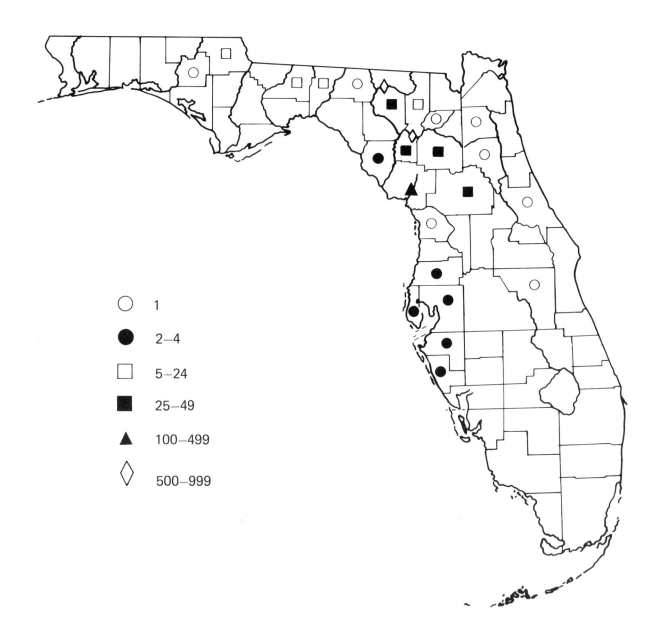

Map 2. Distribution of projectile points from the Late Paleo period.

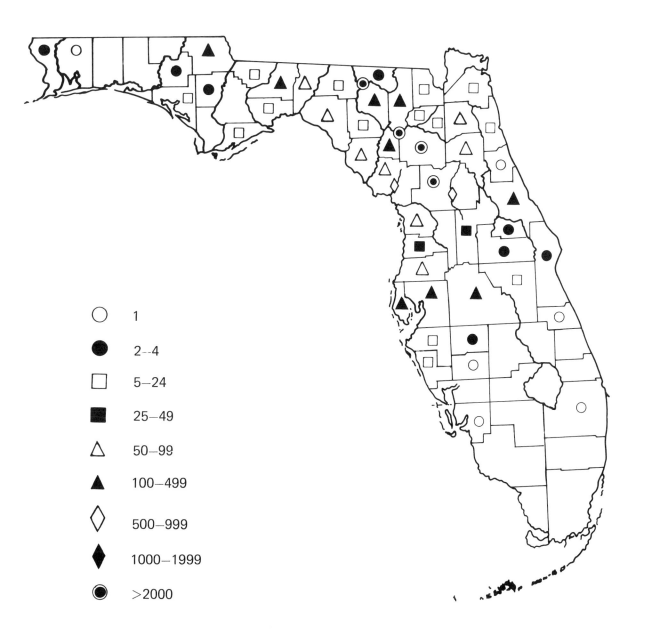

Map 3. Distribution of projectile points from the Preceramic Archaic period.

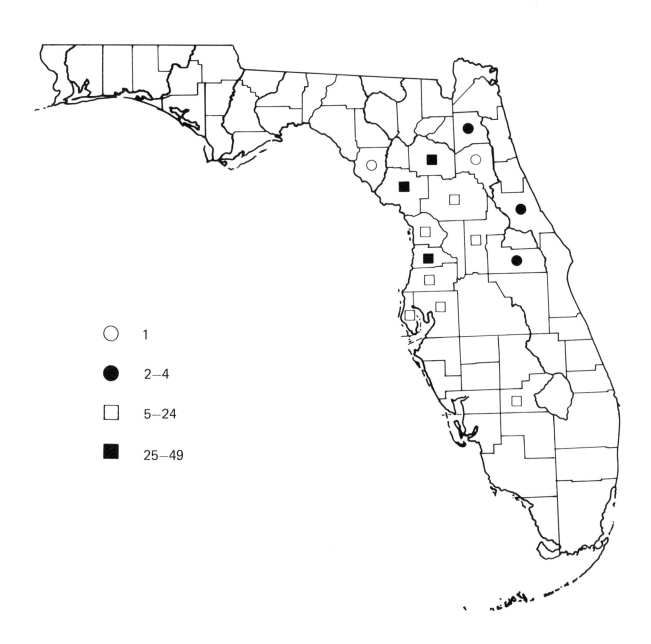

Map 4. Distribution of basally notched points from the Early Ceramic period.

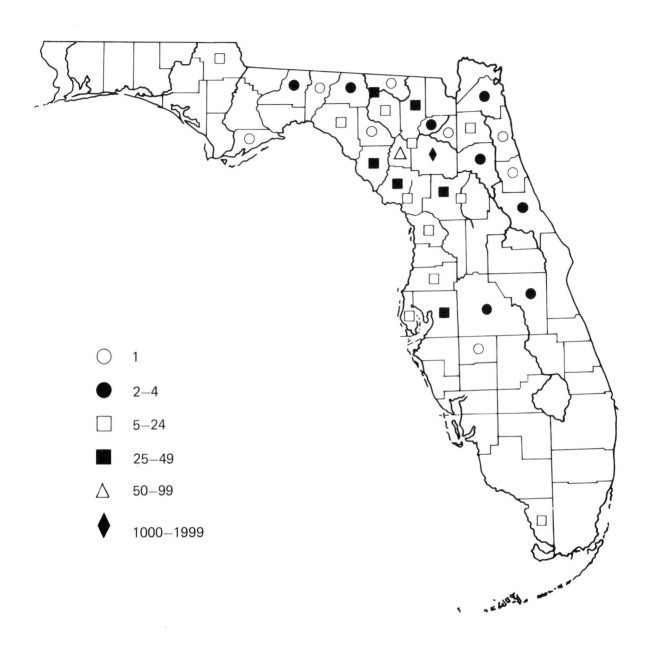

Legend

- ○ 1
- ● 2–4
- □ 5–24
- ■ 25–49
- △ 50–99
- ◆ 1000–1999

Map 5. Distribution of projectile points from the Late Ceramic period.

recent times. The number diminishes and for the most part the workmanship degenerates. Map 5 indicates that more of these points are found in Alachua County than any other county, but the significance of this fact is reduced by recognition that Alachua County has been extensively investigated. With time the number of points recovered from the rivers decreases. The distribution of stone artifacts in the Late Ceramic is not as broad as in the Preceramic Archaic period except for an unexplained occurrence of points in Monroe County.

For all time periods, most of the points have been recovered in close proximity to chert outcrops. Since few stone implements have been found in the southern part of the state, this suggests that stone was not traded nor did people living in places like South Florida travel far to utilize stone sources.

THREE
Stoneworking Technology

The fabrics of a people unlock their social history. They speak a language which is silent but yet more eloquent than the written page.

(Snyder 1881:563)

A comprehensive investigation of any technology includes an account of its origins. But stoneworking technology has existed since the time of the Australopithecines, who lived in Africa about two million years ago. That was so long before recorded history that speculation must accompany any attempt to determine how these people initially decided that flint was the most desirable material for stone implements, how they knew where to find the flint, how they determined that the flint available was satisfactory for their needs, how they developed techniques to use it efficiently, and how they adjusted their seasonal migrations for stops at quarries and stoneworking activities. We know from evidence at Olduvai Gorge (Leakey 1971) in eastern Africa that Australopithecines were altering stones to create crude implements. It seems evident that early humanlike creatures noticed that some broken rocks in a streambed had sharp cutting edges or that certain rocks used as pounding instruments broke at an angle that left a sharp edge suitable for cutting (Bordaz 1970:8–9; Bordes 1968:44; Oakley 1972:13).

67

Stoneworking Technology

Presumably, the advantages of cutting with a hard, durable material with predictable fracture properties eventually became apparent, and a long, slow process of technological development began. At first there were no traditions to fall back on and no neighbors from whom to borrow new ideas. Sons learned from fathers, generation after generation, and the technical changes adopted in their tools are now perceptible to archaeologists in studies of the progressive development of stone tool technology.

Possibly Oakley is correct in stating that "in the Paleolithic and Mesolithic periods man obtained flint mainly from the banks and beds of rivers or from cliffs and sea-beaches. In the Neolithic stage he learned to follow good quality flint underground" (Oakley 1972:19). Few systematic studies have been conducted of Old World quarries and their utilization may be older than is presently apparent. Early stoneworkers must have developed excellent rockhound sense, enabling them to recognize the most desirable quality of stone for their needs. Knowles (1953:93) relates that in Australia to this day a hunter always keeps his eyes open for useful bits of stone to make spearheads: "He will take up a piece of broken rock, the size of his fist, lying on the surface of the ground, and test it by striking it with any convenient lump of stone lying about that will serve as a hammer. He will knock pieces off the edges of the stone he has noticed. If it flakes nicely he will break it down to somewhere near the size of a spear-head, and put it in his paper-bark wallet, to be dressed into shape at his leisure in his camp."

By the time people arrived in the Western Hemisphere from the Old World, before 20,000 years ago, they had probably already solved most of the basic problems pertaining to stoneworking technology.

Chert
resources

Little notice was taken by the early pioneers in any part of America of the aboriginal industries connected with the quarrying and shaping of stone (Holmes 1919:155).

Quarry areas in
Florida

Holmes's monumental volume is the only inclusive account of the quarrying and mining procedures of aboriginal Americans.

68

Although considered incomplete by the modern archaeologist, it remains an important reference source. Holmes does not discuss the ages when the quarries were utilized, he does not include a study of the chipping debris, nor does he mention the sources of Florida cherts. It was not possible for Holmes to consider these details since the only information available in 1919 was the following paragraphs about Florida that appeared in the *Annual Report of the Smithsonian Institution* for 1879 under the heading "Ancient Arrow-Head Factory":

About five miles south of the Kootie River, and some two miles north of the mouth of Anclote River, is a small stream called Trouble Creek. A considerable body of blue flint-rock occurs here, cropping out along the shores of the creek, with scattering nodules lying in all directions. This point was evidently used for a long time by the aborigines as a factory for arrow and spear heads. Bushels of chips and fragments strew the ground, and large quantities have been washed from the banks of the creek and cover its bottom. A long search revealed nothing except a few arrow points and spear heads spoiled in making, and a lot of broken pottery.

No doubt excavations along the banks would bring other relics to light, as the Indians must have resorted to this place in large numbers, and have worked here for a long series of years, judging from the depth of soil over the chips (Walker 1879:394).

In the Third Biennial Report of the Florida State Board of Conservation (1939:63–64), there is an article entitled "Aboriginal Stone Quarries of Hillsborough County and Sources of Abrasives and Pigment." The anonymous author of this article (possibly J. Clarence Simpson) discusses the abundance of silicified coral and chert remains and the evidence of intensive quarrying operations. The writer states that the method employed in quarrying was shallow trenching and pitting, and he or she goes on to say that large boulders were broken and fractured on the spot by the use of fire and that the fragments were further reduced by striking with any convenient stone at hand. The material was roughed out into suitable flakes and blanks to be finished elsewhere.

Simpson (1941:32– 34) provides the most comprehensive account of stone resource areas for Florida aboriginal artifacts, mentioning quarries in Pinellas, Jefferson, Alachua, and Hillsborough counties. Quarrying, according to Simpson, was accomplished by digging shallow trenches and pits. Fire was used to break the stones into rough shapes, after which they were further worked by hammering into blanks that were carried away to be finished. He further notes that the word *Thonotosassa* used to name a Hillsborough County lake is a Muscogean word meaning "flint place."

In Florida, chert suitable for stone tool production is available along the courses of many rivers and crops out at the surface in areas where limestone has been dissolved away, allowing the siliceous bodies to project from the surrounding terrain in ridges and mounds (fig. 29). Situations exist in Florida similar to those described by Holmes at Flint Ridge, Ohio, but quarrying in Florida is vastly easier since the chert is not deeply buried and erosion has exceeded deposit in most places.

Figure 29. Outcrop of Florida chert.

. . . the digger attacked the clays that result from the disintegration of the limestone. All the lime has been dissolved by the humic and carbonic acids carried downward by percolating waters which, however, have no effect on the flint, and the nodules are left scattered throughout the clay much in the order as that in which they occurred in the limestone (Holmes 1919:185).

As recently as 1949 when *Archaeology of the Florida Gulf Coast* was published, Willey had the following to say about stone remains: "Projectiles and large lance points were met with in many of the burial mounds. Some of these were large beautifully chipped ceremonial blades. They could have been made of native flint. There is little information on point forms. . . . Moore offers few illustrations or descriptions of chipped-stone material" (Willey 1949:393). In Plates 54*a*, 55, 56, and 57 of Willey's book, projectile points now known to belong to the Paleo Indian, Late Paleo, Preceramic Archaic, and Ceramic periods are listed as Safety Harbor period artifacts (A.D. 1200). Obviously, points of a number of time periods were mixed when they were scooped up and deposited with mound fill. Willey does not include a table of stone tool types nor does he mention the abundance of available stone sources in some of the Gulf Coast counties. It is apparent that the preoccupation at that time was with ceramics rather than with stone remains of Florida, and it is clear that Willey has not written the final word about Florida Gulf Coast archaeology, inasmuch as conclusions are still lacking about the tool types and the chert sources utilized.

A number of areas have been identified where material suitable for producing chipped stone implements was utilized. These include many locations in the Tampa Bay area and east and northeast of there to Zephyrhills; along the Aucilla, Econfina, Fenholloway, Suwannee, and Santa Fe rivers; the Withlacoochee River flowing south from Georgia to Florida; the Kanapaha (Hemmings and Kohler 1974) and York (Purdy 1977) sites in Alachua County; the Johnson Lake (Bullen and Dolan 1959), Container Corporation of

71

Stoneworking Technology

America (Purdy 1981*a*), and Edwards (Purdy 1975*a*) sites in Marion County.

Few systematic and no complete studies have yet been conducted of any lithic procurement sites in Florida. Many of these sites have been destroyed by the construction of housing or shopping centers or they have been extensively vandalized by amateur collectors. (Since they are already on the endangered list, the precise locations of the chert sources of Florida are not given in this volume. A list of quarry sites is on file at the University of Florida.)

Quarry
procedures

The actual process of quarrying is rather varied (Gould et al. 1971:160).

Apparently early explorers took no notice of stone procurement practices in Florida. In order to develop theories about quarrying in prehistoric Florida, it is necessary to resort to descriptions from other parts of the world and to compare findings from their quarry sites with those reported from Florida sites.

Lithic technologists and researchers employ three methods to study ways early stoneworkers extracted and worked lithic raw materials: (1) systematic investigations of stone debitage at sites where procurement and reduction took place; (2) observations of techniques still being used by the few stone tool–making peoples remaining in the world today; (3) replication experiments, which provide valuable insights into the problems faced by early stoneworkers and can, by extrapolation, be used to analyze manufacturing and utilization techniques employed by prehistoric peoples.

The most complete investigation of flintknapping was made of the gunflint industry at Brandon, England (Clarke 1935; and his cited references). Clarke speaks of geographic and geologic availability of the flint, mining techniques, implements employed, selection for quality, historic continuity, and supply and demand. He observed that flintknapping is restricted to a few families among whom intermarriage was "more than common" (Clarke 1935:44). Of

72

further interest is his statement that "knappers die before the age of 40 from consumption caused by the inhalation of flint particles" (p. 52). An idiosyncratic technical vocabulary and bookkeeping system preserved by miners and knappers are described, providing clues about the antiquity of the industry. Important also is the information about the number of gunflints that can be produced.

A knapper of average skill can produce from 5,000 to 7,000 flakes in a day, while an expert has struck as many as 10,000 in the same time. Flints can be knapped at the rate of 300 per hour, though slightly more have been completed by knappers of outstanding proficiency. This daily total of 2,500 gunflints is exclusive of the flakes used as raw material. . . . In 1868 the total weekly output was 200,000–250,000 gunflints (Clarke 1935:53–54).

It is no wonder that two million years of flint-working activities have resulted in hundreds of thousands of stone tools and inestimable amounts of debitage.

The account of the Brandon flintknappers furnishes a valuable description of quarrying procedures that may be partially applicable to the Florida situation. Picks, hammers, spades, and crowbars, for instance, probably were similar, differing primarily only in the material of which they were made. Florida's early stoneworkers, however, did not have to dig shafts 10 or more meters deep to reach quality stone, nor did they use exclusively the sophisticated blade technique necessary in the gunflint industry.

Holmes (1919) discusses stone quarries throughout North America. The procedures involved in quarrying were as varied as the geographic and geologic locations. Pits, vertical shafts, and horizontal tunneling are all mentioned, with fire, stone, antler picks, mauls, sledges, and hammerstones used to break up the stone. The discussion about the use of fire in breaking up massive strata and more intractable bodies of rock is intriguing, "but the extent of its application in the mining work can only be conjectured" (p. 156).

Stoneworking Technology

Holmes cites the investigations of Gerald Fowke at Flint Ridge, Ohio, where Fowke speculates that:

> He then sunk a pit, as large as he wished, to the surface of the flint. On this he made a fire; and when the stone was hot he threw water on it, causing it to shatter. Throwing aside the fragments, he repeated the process until he penetrated the underlying limestone to a depth which allowed him sufficient room to work conveniently. The top and freshly made face of the flint was thickly plastered with potter's clay, after which fire and water were again utilized for clearing away the limestone until a cavity was formed beneath the flint layer. Thus a projecting ledge would be left from which the burnt parts were knocked off with heavy stone hammers until the unaltered flint was exposed (Holmes 1919:177)(fig. 30).

An experiment conducted a number of years ago at Flint Ridge may cast some doubt on the use of fire in quarrying operations. In the experiment, after a fire of intense heat was kindled on the underlying surface of the flint, two buckets of cold water were thrown on the stone, which did not break into large pieces as

Figure 30. Quarrying at Flint Ridge, Ohio (from Holmes 1919:177).

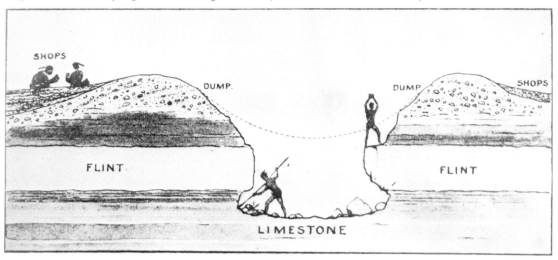

expected but checked and cracked to a depth of half an inch (Ellis 1940:45).

It is clear from the statement of Fowke and from the result of Ellis's experiment that "fire is destructive to stone and if not very discreetly employed will so flaw the stone as to make it unfit for most uses" (Holmes 1919:364).

I recently completed (Purdy 1981*b*) an extensive literature review to determine whether there are firsthand accounts describing the use of fire at flint quarries. Only two reports were found: one, about the Wintu tribe of Indians in the northern Sacramento Valley who "split off blocks of obsidian at Glass Mountain by building a fire against the rock" (Dubois 1939:127; Heizer and Treganza 1944:302). A second account relates that the Alyawara Aborigines of central Australia use fire to break up blocks of quartzite. The fire is allowed to burn for only a few minutes until the block begins to crack (O'Connell 1979:personal communication).

The literature review reveals that the firesetting technique, as an aid to breaking rocks in mining metal ores, is very ancient and persisted even after the invention of explosives in 1627. Water was sometimes poured on the heated surface to hasten the action. Firesetting was used to remove overburden or destroy the matrix in which ore was encased.

I conducted a firesetting experiment at the Container Corporation of America site in Marion County, Florida. A large tabular piece of chert was selected. Dry grass and yellow lighter pine were placed on the surface of the stone and ignited. Two pyrometers were used and probes were inserted into the center of the wood fire where they reached a maximum temperature of 850°C. The probes were then placed directly on the rock surface where the temperature remained fairly constant at 720°C. Within 20 minutes after the fire was kindled, the rock began to crack—this was apparent both visibly and audibly. Fragments exfoliated forcefully for a distance greater than 8 meters. Fifteen minutes later the wood was removed and a large chert nodule was thrown at the heated slab, which fractured easily. Water was then poured over the heated stone, which caused it to sizzle and steam. The chert nodule was thrown again at the slab, and the slab literally disintegrated. Later, an attempt was made to flake a piece of the stone with a soft hammer (moose antler) but the stone fell apart (Purdy 1981*b*).

My conclusion from the literature review and from the field experiment is that it would not have been advantageous to use the firesetting technique to obtain siliceous materials for the production of chipped stone implements. Since direct fire is destructive to rock, firesetting would have to have been very carefully controlled (as done by the Australian Aborigines) or employed primarily to remove unwanted material in order to expose quality flint. Firesetting to destroy silica materials was extensively and beneficially used in mining and quarrying operations. The field experiment conducted at the CCA site illustrated that approximately seven to eight feet of unwanted material can be demolished in an 8-hour period using the firesetting technique followed by a cold water bash.

Of more application to the Florida situation is Holmes's comment that in boulder and nodule quarries—where the matrix was sand, clay, or gravel—stone picks and antler points were used in penetrating the deposits. Additional observations by Holmes and other investigators about quarries pertain to the quantity of rejected material, quarry ownership, and activities other than extraction. Because of its limestone topography, the Florida landscape is pitted with sinkholes in which a sequence of geologic deposits can be seen, including strata containing chert. It is possible that these naturally occurring pits were widened by primitive people seeking quality chert not yet weathered by exposure. Many large stone picks have been found at the CCA and Edwards sites in Marion County that would have served as ideal instruments for removing the stone from its matrix of sandy clay. Primitive people may also have used antler picks for this purpose, but none have survived.

All accounts describing the appearance of quarry areas mention the amount of waste material found there. Fowke says, "probably nine-tenths of the flint carried from the pits . . . was rejected" (Holmes 1919:178). Bryan states that "in the study of the great flint

quarries one should expect to find large quantities of waste rock"
(1950:33). Singer and Ericson (1977:183–85) used 5,000 years of
accumulated debitage to calculate biface manufacture at an obsidian
quarry in California. Gould observes that:

> If the cherty material occurs as nodules on the surface of the
> ground, the Aborigine takes a small boulder and uses it to smash
> a few nodules. He selects the flakes he wants from the resulting
> piles of chippings and debris. Working in this way, a man can
> leave behind as many as two hundred waste flakes for each flake
> he actually chooses. Behavior like this accounts for the
> tremendous quantities of unused stone flakes which one
> characteristically finds on the surface of aboriginal quarries
> (Gould et al. 1971:160-61).

Although chert procurement areas of Florida are similar to those
elsewhere in the amount of chipping material they contain, closer
examination of total debitage recovered during excavations in Florida
has provided interesting data. For example, from one 3-meter square
at the CCA site in Marion County that yielded over 10,000 stone
remains, it appears that after the stone was uncovered by early men
and women, they sometimes used the block-on-block technique to
break up the huge nodules or tabular chert (both occur in Florida).
From a different level of the same square, however, every piece of
stone included a striking platform, a bulb of percussion, and a fairly
uniform shape. The most interesting result of the examination of this
site is that 12 percent of the systematically struck and 15 percent of
the shattered material exhibited use wear even though only two
bifacially flaked implements were recovered. This observation
demonstrates that not all debitage is rejected material and that a time
factor probably explains differences in techniques employed to reduce
the large nodules and tabular chert. Bryan argues that quarry sites
did not exist solely for the production of exportable material. He
asserts that many quarries were industrial sites where a variety of
articles were made. The evidence in Florida substantiates Bryan's
contention that "for the manufacture by primitives of articles of wood

or bone on a large scale, large quantities of flint tools are required. For economy of effort, it is necessary to balance the carrying of the raw material to the flint or the flint to the raw material" (Bryan 1950:20–21). Based on ethnographic accounts describing material items used by Florida Indians, it is possible to speculate that activities at quarry sites, other than projectile point manufacture, included the production of canoes, clubs (macanas), spear and arrow shafts, bows, basketry, religious and other works of art (i.e., carvings such as the famous owl and eagle totems and the Key Marco specimens), and bone tools. A full range of stone implements is found at outcrop work sites, including choppers to cut down trees, a variety of adzes and scrapers to shape wood and bone, and burins that could be used to make incisions on all materials, including human skin in preparation for the tattooing of nobles, the results of which are pictured by le Moyne (fig. 31). An observation made at the Senator Edwards chipped stone work site that has not been treated extensively in the literature is the evidence of novices' attempts at toolmaking. Symmetry and uniformity of flake removal are essential for the production of projectile points. Specimens were examined whose flaking was crude with symmetry not maintained, yet they could be classified only as poorly made points. Apprenticeship must have occurred somewhere, and it is logical that it should be evident at a workshop site.

Data from Florida sites tend to confirm several facts.

(1) Formal tools were made in Florida at places other than quarries (Gould et al. 1971:161; Holmes 1919:178; Simpson 1941:32–34). How far away? At the CCA and Edwards sites, the distance could have been a few meters. Areas where final reduction took place are characterized by the recovery of (a) increased numbers of projectile points, (b) fine chipping debris not found at the procurement site, and (c) thermally altered flakes. (Thermal alteration, discussed in chapter four, is a technique used primarily to facilitate the production of projectile points.) In addition to the three characteristics listed, a dramatic decrease occurred in the weight of the chipping debris, confirming that initial stages of reduction had occurred at a place other than the

Figure 31. Tattooing (from the engravings of le Moyne; Bennett 1968: 38).

finishing site. For example, in the square yielding over 10,000 stone artifacts at the CCA site, the total weight was 206,053 grams, not including the large nodules left at the sites (an average of about 20 grams for each specimen). In another square, 4,069 artifacts were recovered weighing 16,629 grams (an average of 4 grams each). The second square yielded 29 percent of the total artifact recovery of the two squares but only 7 percent of the weight. Twelve projectile points, other bifaces, scrapers, utilized flakes, and fine chipping debris, including heat-altered flakes, were found in the second square.

Interpretation of the information from the CCA site supports the conclusion, reached also by Bryan (1950), that if a quarry were in a location where other needed resources were available, living areas would be identified close by.

(2) For many tasks, shape is not as important as a functional edge. The New Guineans "use a piece of stone for a particular task if particular features of it make it suitable for the work in hand. The idea that formal patterning of tools is relatively unimportant is clearly supported by the ethnographic study which shows that the stone tool makers place primary stress on the functional edge" (White 1967). Gould et al. (1971:156) concur that a hand axe sometimes consists of nothing more than a hand-held rock with a sharp edge, picked up off the ground when needed and thrown away after use. To make his point Gould cites a now classic photograph illustrated in Oakley (1972:6) of a hand axe shown in use by an Australian Aborigine.

After an examination of 70,000 chert remains from a trench dug at the Edwards site, Marion County, Florida, I concluded that a distinction should be made between "convenience" tools and "future use" tools (Purdy 1975a:183). At the CCA site (Purdy 1977) it was observed that stone remains with no patterned shape did exhibit similar use wear. In other words, although overall morphology was not classifiable, the objects could be classified according to function.

(3) Use wear on stone remains may not always be apparent. A number of recent studies have demonstrated that no edge damage can be detected after rather rigorous application of stone to materials

such as wood and bone. Variables considered were the types of wood (hard or soft), the condition of bone (green or seasoned), the properties of the stone used to perform the task, the length of time involved, and many other aspects such as method of holding the stone and the material being worked (Crabtree and Davis 1968; Tringham et al. 1974; Gould et al. 1971; Stafford 1977). A statement by Gould will suffice to make the point.

> Following traditional Aborigine motor patterns, the hafted
> adze was drawn firmly along a shaft of mulga (*Acacia aneura*)
> wood for 1,000 strokes without any resharpening. The working
> edge of the tool was then re-examined under the microscope,
> and a total of eight small terminated flakes was discovered.
> Further use of the tool in this manner would doubtless have
> given rise to more of these use-wear flakes (Gould et al. 1971:160).

But most untrimmed flakes are "not used long enough to cause any appreciable wear" (Gould et al. 1971:163). Crabtree and Davis conclude that dulling of a stone tool often was caused by clogging of its edge with crushed wood fiber and that use-flakes were generally accidentally produced when stone tools were used improperly (1968:428).

At the CCA Site in Marion County, Florida, where use wear can be discerned on 15 percent of the untrimmed flakes, it can probably be assumed that many more were used that show no wear at all and no patterned use scars, making positive interpretation impossible.

(4) Reuse can occur to complicate an analysis of waste material. In Australia, "there is a tendency for people sometimes to pick up ancient stone tools from the surface of sites where they are camped and re-use these implements. Small finely-made backed blades and flakes of chert occur on the surface of many old campsites, and recent stratigraphic work near Warburton has shown that these tools definitely pre-date the present culture of the region" (Gould et al. 1971:163). Singer and Ericson noticed that "artifacts from later sites are often reworked pieces or utilized fragments of larger bifacially flaked implements" (1977:186).

Stoneworking Technology

At the Florida sites, many deeply weathered artifacts have been restruck, resulting in differential patina where fresh flake scars occur. Weathering takes time, and the most likely explanation for the unequal weathering is that discarded implements were reused. Goodwin (1961) has also reached this conclusion.

(5) Early peoples recognized flint of good quality for tool making. Gerald Fowke observed at a quarry site in Missouri that:

> As a rule the digging was done along the lowest part of the deposit. This is because the upper layers, being more influenced by weathering are less suitable for making implements. The most exposed portions are porous from the weathering out of fossils and are also much checked and seamed so that they easily shatter. . . . Judging from the amount of waste in the form of spalls and blocks covering the hillsides below, a vast quantity of chert was removed and thrown aside in order to reach that which had desirable flaking qualities. After long exposure most of it resembles chalk . . . (Holmes 1919:195).

Chert recovered at the York site (8-A1-480), Alachua County, Florida, displayed no evidence of utilization. It was concluded that:

> Florida chert, outcropping or immediately under the surface in a well-drained terrain would eventually lose some adsorbed water. . . . The elevation of the York site is about 37 m above the mean sea level. Most of the diagnostic stone remains recovered in the surrounding area were found at 23–30 m. If the elevation falls much below 23 m in this part of Florida, the land will be under water. At the lower elevations, therefore, chert material would be found in deposits with greater moisture and probably would be more highly selected.
>
> The chert from the York site was very "dry" and fossiliferous. Attempts to flake it resulted in step fractures and, eventually, failure by end shock. . . .
>
> In addition to dryness, the chert lacked other desirable qualities, i.e., homogeneity and small grain size. If better quality

materials in more convenient locations had not been available, the chert from the York site probably would have sufficed (Purdy 1977:7).

These conclusions are not the final word, however, because certain types of weathering can obliterate flake scars and use wear. If a time factor is included in quarry site analysis, new dimensions are introduced that might lead to a reconsideration of previous interpretations. For instance, rock exposed at the surface today may have been buried previously under a different set of environmental conditions and thus protected from weathering.

Ancient ownership of quarries and trading of the raw materials are mentioned by several authors. As previously noted, the practice of mining among the Brandon flintworkers is restricted to a few families (Clarke 1935:44). In California, the control of quarries was "tribal but related and nearby groups had the right to quarry either freely or on the payment of small gifts. Wars resulted from attempts by distant tribes to use a quarry without payment. On the other hand, the Clear Lake obsidian quarries . . . were neutral ground" (Bryan 1950:34). The famous red pipestone quarry in Minnesota, according to George Catlin, "was held and owned in common, and as a neutral ground amongst the different tribes who met here to renew their sacred calumets under some superstition which stayed the tomahawk of natural foes always raised in deadly hate and vengeance in other places" (Holmes 1919:262). The United States, in a treaty ratified in 1858, specified that the Yancton Sioux had unrestricted use of the red pipestone quarry for the purpose of procuring stone for pipes. In 1859, one square mile, including the quarry, was surveyed as a reservation (Holmes 1919:262–63). As recently as 1900, the Sioux visited the pipestone quarry yearly. Flint Ridge, Ohio, is thought to have been neutral ground from which the raw material was carried away or traded because it is found at sites throughout a wide area. An analysis of the material from Bodie Hills, California, verified that export of obsidian into central and southern California began well before 2000 B.C.: "Partially finished bifaces and complete unmodified

Quarry owners and users

83

prismatic blades were products carried away from the quarry workshops and distributed within consumer areas. . . . " (Singer and Ericson 1977:171). Gould says there are many localities with chert-like stone suitable for making chipped implements near the Warburton Ranges in Australia that are well known to the Aborigines, but they also use detrital and insolation flakes found almost everywhere in their country. Gould gives no indication of any concept of quarry site ownership on the part of the Aborigines. In fact, he mentions that the chipping of stone tools is regarded as an art of little importance. It is of interest, however, that different colors are preferred by certain groups, not because of chipping quality but because of the close totemic ties each man has to the particular region in which he was born and from which he claims totemic descent.

> Thus, a man may have a sense of kinship with some of the localities, and he will value the stone material from them as part of his own being. Stone materials thus acquired are not sacred in any strict sense but are nevertheless valued highly enough to be transported over long distances by the owners. . . . Situations like this made it easier to understand how materials can be found occurring on sites many miles from the localities where they were quarried or collected (Gould et al. 1971:160–63).

Such observations provide new levels of analysis.

A clue to quarry rights in Florida comes from the Senator Edwards site (Purdy 1975a), where at least eight different varieties of Preceramic Archaic stemmed projectile points were recovered. Some varieties exist in a single time period; thus it is possible to deduce that autonomous but related groups had access to the same raw material, i.e., from neutral ground. Ethnographic data support this concept of nonprivate ownership of property among hunting-gathering groups. With the knowledge presently available, any other statement about quarry ownership in Florida is merely speculation. It is not likely, however, that stone procurement areas in Florida were ever jealously guarded even when a higher socioeconomic level was reached about 2,000 years ago. There was no production of large ceremonial blades like those associated with cultures in other parts of North America (California, Tennessee, Mesoamerica, Ohio Valley), which necessitated specialized crafts and central control of quarries. In fact, it appears that stoneworking actually declined in Florida following the Preceramic Archaic period and was partially replaced by the use of implements manufactured from other materials such as shell.

Chert procurement practices varied depending upon the time period, the socioeconomic level of the group, and the availability of raw material. If most of the problems associated with stoneworking had been solved before people entered the Western Hemisphere, as we believe they were, many of the statements made about the use of stone in modern stone age cultures, with modification, can be applied to prehistoric Florida. Early Floridians, for example, could easily obtain good quality chert materials, and visits to quarries were probably routine. According to Gould et al. (1971:160) the Australian Aborigines visit quarries often. Recent ethnographic observations of stone tool manufacture and use in Ethiopia revealed that:

> Trips to the quarry are made on foot and the quarry may be up to a half-day's walk from the village. The frequency of trips to the quarry ranges from once every 15 days to once every two or three months. The quarries do not seem to be owned or controlled by any individual or group. There is some trading . . . that takes place between people who live close to quarries and those who are more distant (Gallagher 1977:408–9).

The Indians living in north-central Florida would not have had to travel far to a stone outcrop, but few stone implements are found at sites with no nearby outcrops. This situation suggests that there was no great exportation of material as reported for other places such as Flint Ridge.

Because stone artifacts are preserved through time and are present at quarry sites in large numbers, study of the stone remains from these areas can provide information about the time periods when the quarries were used.

85

Stoneworking Technology

Recent discoveries at the Container Corporation of America site in Marion County may provide proof that people were in Florida prior to the Paleo Indian period. At the site there are two soil horizons: (1) an upper sand zone containing recognizable stone artifacts dating from the Paleo Indian Period, 12,000 years ago to A.D. 1000 and (2) a lower sandy clay zone containing crude stone implements that are very weathered and technologically so distinct from the tools in the overlying sand that no cultural continuity is evident. The extreme differences in technology and weathering of the stone implements from the two soil horizons suggests that there was a long temporal break in human occupation at the site.

I am convinced by the field situation that the artifacts from the sandy clay horizon are ancient, but the stone implements and the sandy clay deposit from which they were recovered must be investigated thoroughly before positive statements can be made about their antiquity.

Diagnostic stone implements representing all time periods of Florida's prehistory are found at chert outcrop sites and the greatest utilization appears to have been during the Preceramic Archaic period.

Quarry site analysis has been neglected by archaeologists even though there has been increased interest in lithic technology. One of the most fascinating problems pertaining to quarrying procedures, for example, is determining how huge slabs, nodules, or blocks of stone were broken into small pieces for flaking. Wilfrid Jury has conducted the only study I know of in which an investigator actually used techniques and implements available to primitive people to accomplish the task of fracturing large boulders.

Near the outcrop was found a crushing site near an old tree stump at which chert fragments or slabs 12 to 18 inches in length and several inches thick surrounded granite blocks 10 to 12 inches in diameter. By experiment, Jury showed that a lever 24 feet long held under the roots of a large tree and brought down by four men on a large flint-block laid on one of the

86

granite blocks would crush the flint into slabs of the appropriate size and shape (Bryan 1950:27).

Despite the fact that we are often in the dark about what was really being produced at quarries, we can determine much more about lithic techniques, technology, and typology at quarry sites than we can by studying lithic remains from other types of archaeological sites. In fact, the typically excavated archaeological site is the worst possible location for studies of lithic technologies. On the other hand, a thorough examination of outcrop and working areas provides data pertaining to (1) quarrying procedures, (2) the roughing out of implements—the preliminary dressing of stone, (3) tools such as anvils and hammerstones used to perform quarrying tasks, (4) leftover materials such as spent cores and chipping debris. Study in these four areas, especially the last one, is often more informative than a study of completed tools. A disadvantage of studying debitage at quarry sites is that evidence of an implement's long-time or extreme use is not usually found because with unlimited amounts of raw materials available toolmakers may be presumed to have discarded dulled flakes rather than resharpening them because they were so easily replaced.

Because chipping flint is a reductive process, we can find artifacts in all stages of manufacture at quarries and determine step by step how these artifacts were being produced there even if we do not know their use. Metallurgy was invented before people had exhausted all available flint resources. Otherwise, they might have had to utilize every scrap of stone and resharpen and reuse implements discarded generations earlier.

. . . the men congregated in a circle, in a warm sunny place, painted their faces with black mud to keep the flying flakes out of their eyes, and maintained silence—either for ceremonial purposes or to avoid getting pieces of flint or glass in the mouth (Pope 1918:117).

Chert reduction techniques

Stoneworking Technology

Introduction to
reduction
techniques

A number of accurate, complete records and experimental studies have been done on the flintworking techniques used to produce task-specific stone implements—for instance there exist very good first-hand descriptions of knappers manufacturing projectile points. The best known observation of a North American flintworker is the account of Ishi, the last surviving Yahi Indian who wandered into Oroville, California, in 1910 (Pope 1918; Kroeber 1961).

Although traditional ways of making and using chipped stone tools have diminished around the world and soon will disappear altogether, detailed studies and descriptions of stone utilization and function have been made by Gould (1968, et al. 1971) among the Australian Aborigines and by White (1967) among the people of New Guinea. Accounts of more specialized stone implement manufacture are available about the Brandon flintknappers (Clarke 1935) and about the Turks (Bordaz 1969).

Replication experiments, particularly since the mid-1960s, have provided valuable information about the technology associated with producing chipped stone implements. The most outstanding authority in North America is D.E. Crabtree (1966, 1968, 1970, 1972, and others). Crabtree's observations and the late Earl H. Swanson, Jr.'s foresighted realization that studies of stone tool technology could provide a better understanding of the prehistoric way of life led to the use of lithic studies in archaeological interpretation. Outside of America, Semenov (1964), Bordes (1969a, 1969b), and Tixier (1974) have been influential in encouraging analyses of stone debitage.

Futhermore, in the last decade, instrumental studies have contributed to better understanding of the chemical, physical, and mechanical properties of chert. (For examples see Kerkhof and Muller-Beck 1969; Purdy and Brooks 1971; Faulkner 1972; Speth 1972; Tite 1972; Purdy 1974; Mock 1978; Clark and Purdy 1979a, 1979b; Purdy and Clark 1979; Purdy and Roessler n.d.)
The Bibliography of Archaeology I: Experiments, Lithic Technology, and Petrography (Hester and Heizer 1973) lists hundreds of useful historic and experimental references.

When external forces act upon a rock mass, there are usually two results: the rock is deformed resulting in a change in its shape or size; and internal resisting forces develop in the rock, balancing the externally applied forces. The change in shape or size caused by force is called strain. The intensity of force is called stress. Evaluation of the amount of stress takes into consideration the extent of the area over which the force acts. The smaller the area of applied force, the greater the concentrated effect. When stress exceeds the rock's elastic limits, some degree of rock failure (breakage) results (Nevin 1942).

External forces may result in stress that is tensile, compressive, shearing, bending, torsional, or a combination of these. Chipped stone debitage has been stressed primarily by tensile or shearing forces.

In analyzing lithic remains, it should be kept in mind that only the strained or changed material is recovered; the nature and source of the stress that produced the strain are not known.

The formation of a cone (Hertzian Cone or bulb of force) is the result of force applied to materials which have the property of isotropism, that is, they fracture in the direction of the blow. When force is applied vertically to a flat surface, it will spread, causing a cone to form. The apex of the cone will be truncated in proportion to the surface contacted by the agent transferring the force (Crabtree 1972:54). Chert material fractures isotropically because it has a randomly oriented microcrystalline structure. As a result, a knapper could predict what kind of flake he would obtain depending upon the raw material, the percussor he used, and the force, angle, and velocity of his blow. Each flake is a cone part (fig. 32a). The flake scar left on the parent material is the negative cone part (fig. 32b).

Fracture properties of chert were undoubtedly well understood by the time Florida was inhabited, and the first inhabitants had to adjust their techniques only slightly to accommodate the local material. They probably discovered that Florida chert is larger grained and more fossiliferous than stone material in other regions.

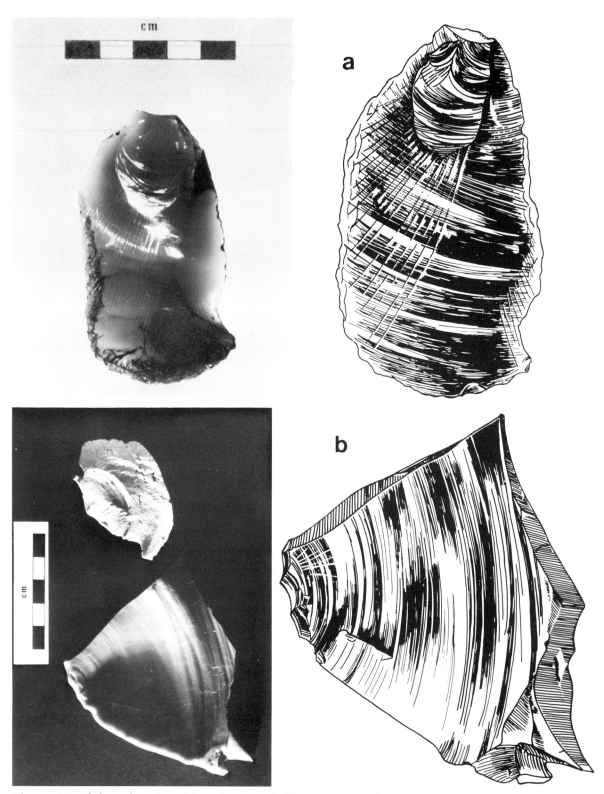

Figure 32. Flakes showing (a) positive and (b) negative bulbs of force.

Fractures of chert materials can be identified as feathered, hinge, step, or split cone. Since breakage characteristics of heat-fractured rock are distinctive, heat-fractured rock can be distinguished from percussion-fractured rock.

Fracture types

A feathered flake terminates with a minimal margin (it "feathers out") and thus is extremely sharp. A lithic technologist would mention feathering as a desirable attribute of an ideal flake. In the evolution of stoneworking technology, it would not have been possible to produce thin bifaces until a technique had been developed to enable a knapper to remove flakes across the face of the implement, thus producing feathered flakes. In order to do this, he had to achieve an admirable balance among material and blow, and he had to be able to produce the same results over and over again in the production of one single finished product.

Feathered fracture

A hinge fracture occurs when chert material is hit with a force in excess of that necessary to detach the flake. A hinge fracture is simple to identify because the flake terminates as a "wave" in the cone part and the break is rounded and smooth (fig. 33). The ventral surface of the flake can be compared to a bivalve shell. Hinge fractures on early stone tools occurred because the knapper was using a hard hammer (stone) or great force or both. In more recent lithic assemblages, hinge fractured flakes might have been struck intentionally to procure a thick short implement with a large striking platform and prominent bulb of force ideally suited for scraping or similar tasks.

Hinge fracture

A step fracture results from an abrupt truncation of a flake as it is being removed. It is caused by a dissipation of force that occurs because not enough force is exerted to detach the flake cleanly or because the stone material is not resilient enough to carry the blow (e.g., is too dry). Step fractures are best identified on the parent rock (fig. 34). In a study of debitage, flakes may be observed that collapsed because of thinness, and these collapsed specimens may be

Step fracture

91

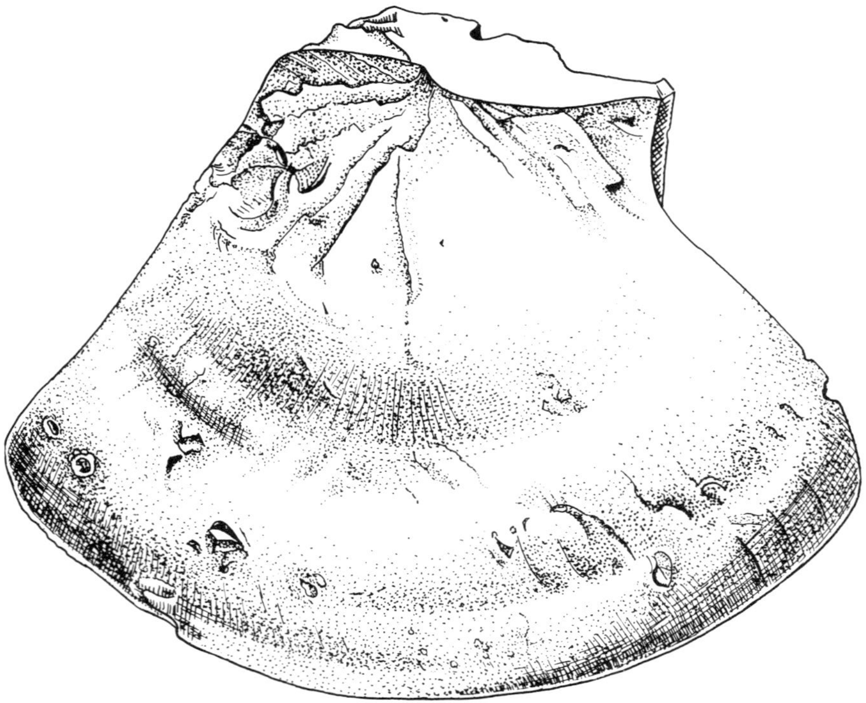

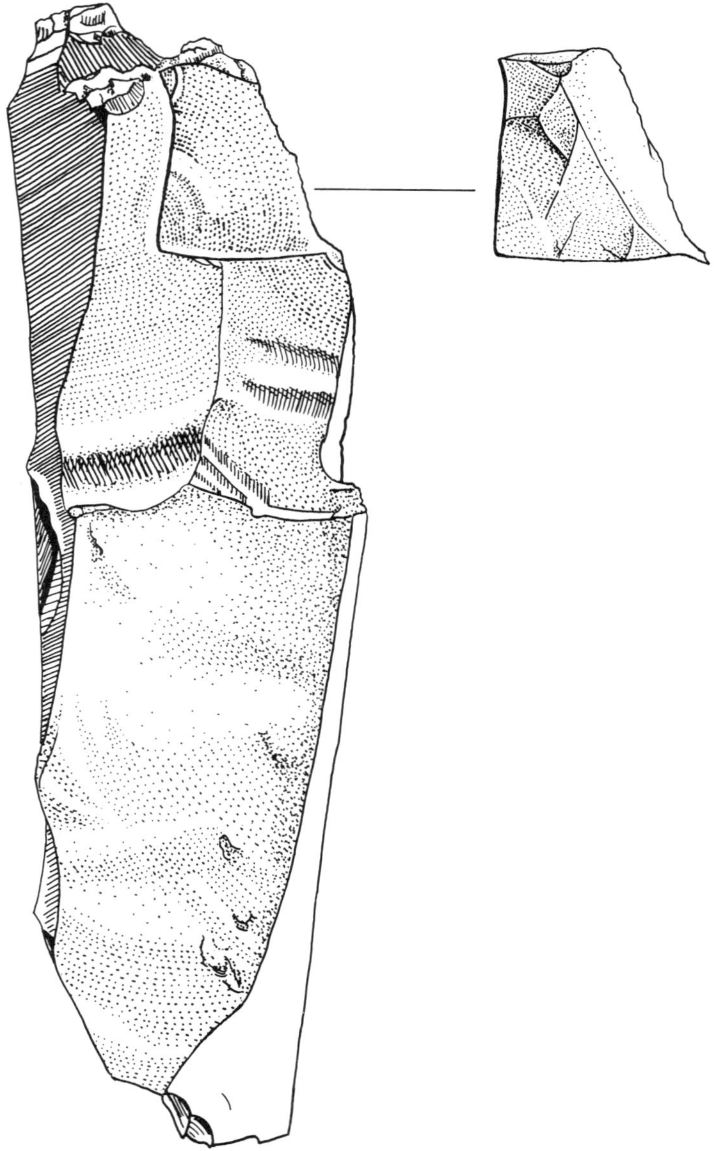

Figure 34. Step fracture.

Figure 33. Hinge fracture.

mistakenly identified as step fractures. It is possible that stoneworkers sometimes intentionally attempted to make flakes "step off" when producing certain implements.

Occasionally, in a study of stone debitage, a flake is found that exhibits no bulb of force. One explanation is that the flake may have been truncated or collapsed and the bulb portion is missing. Another possible explanation is that, in a block-on-block, anvil, or quartering technique, the cone may have been split so that there is no visible cone of percussion. A similar result would occur when the burin technique has been employed to modify a flake or blade by removing the edges parallel, transverse, or oblique to the long axis (Crabtree 1972:48). Another possible explanation for a missing bulb might be lateral snap resulting from end shock when a substantial blow has been imparted to a rock whose mass is not adequately supported to absorb the shock. Since lateral snap does not occur at the point of impact, there is no bulb of force present on the face of the fracture (Purdy 1975*b*). Preston describes the phenomenon as follows:

Split cone

> De Fréminville deals at some length with rupture "par contrecoup," which may perhaps be translated "by repercussion," that is, with ruptures the "foyer d'eclatement" of which is far away from the point where the blow is struck. When the blows are mechanical impacts, it is at first sight striking that the explosion should originate in a totally different region, and from a technical point of view the matter is important; but from a physical standpoint it appears to amount to little more than this, that the area of impact is usually a region of compression, whilst the explosion centre will be in the region of maximum tension. Under suitable conditions, a blow delivered at one point will create a great tension in some other region (Preston 1926:250).

In Florida, many nearly completed, potentially perfect projectile points have been found that broke because of end shock (figs. 35 and 36).

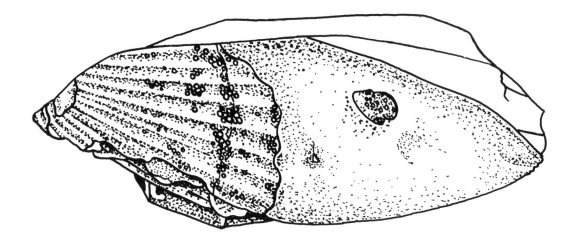

Figure 35. Lateral snap. See also figure 36*a*.

Heat fracture   Although heat fractures do not occur as a direct result of the knapping process, it is important in the interpretation of debitage to recognize them. Florida chert will explode if exposed rapidly to a temperature of 400°C; blocky, angular pieces with "potlids" and no bulbs of force will result. Potlids always occur during the heating process, never during the cooling process (fig. 37). Explosion occurs when the stress that causes decrepitation (the crackling sound that accompanies roasting or calcining of minerals) proceeds too rapidly through the material or exceeds its elastic limits. Florida chert also will explode if heated to 350°C and exposed immediately to room temperature (fig. 38). Thus it appears that explosion by contraction will occur at a lower temperature than explosion by expansion.

The heating required to produce the explosive crack is considerably greater than that needed to allow the formation of the contraction crack on withdrawal of the flame; the contraction crack forms very promptly on such withdrawal (Preston 1926:244).

94

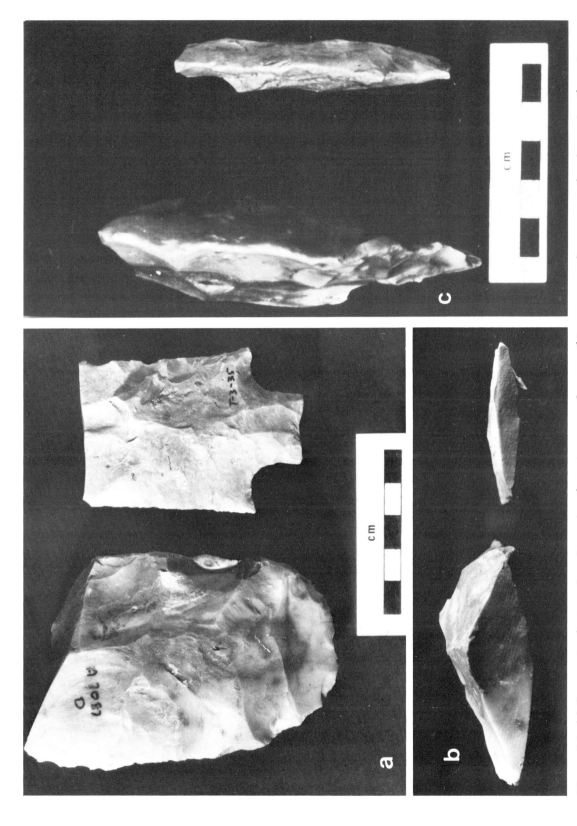

Figure 36. (*a*) Symmetry in top view in projectile point manufacture, (*b*) symmetry in cross section in projectile point manufacture, (*c*) symmetry in lateral view in projectile point manufacture.

Figure 37. Potlid fracture resulting from rapid heating.

Figure 38. Crenated fracture resulting from heat stresses.

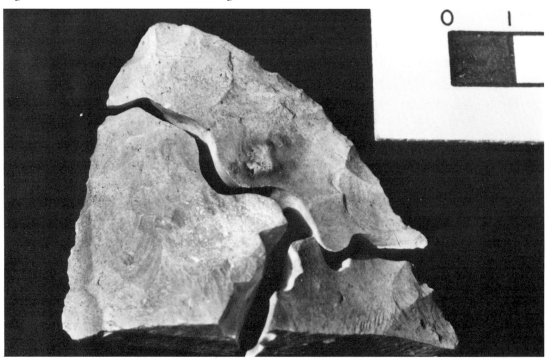

Shrinkage cracks, or crazing, occur if Florida chert is exposed to a temperature above 500°C, even if the temperature is increased very slowly, or if a specimen heated to 400°C is quenched with cold water. These irregular cracks differ in appearance from the normal, smooth conchoidal fracture (fig. 39).

Frost pitting is similar to heat fracture but is hardly applicable to a discussion of Florida chert (Oakley 1972:10).

Chipping flint involves motor skills unfamiliar to modern Americans. There are only two principal ways to detach flakes from cores—by percussion and by pressure; there are two basic types of striking platforms—unprepared and prepared; there are two major classes of percussors—hard hammers such as stone and soft hammers such as antler; and there is one kind of pressure implement.

Flaking

Figure 39. Results of experiment conducted to test the possibility of "flaking" hot stones by dripping cold water on them: *(a)* note the uneven fracture in the center of the picture, *(b)* a magnified area illustrating the crazing which occurred.

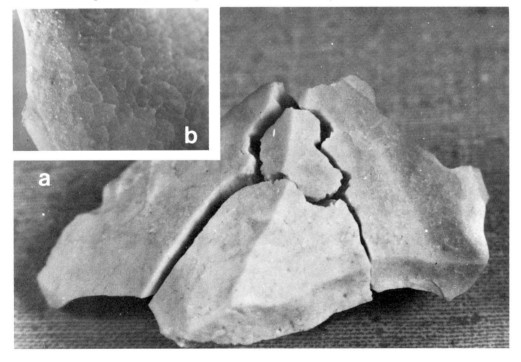

Stoneworking Technology

Percussion techniques

The easiest way to break a rock is to strike it with enough force. There are many variations of percussion techniques, often used in combination.

Direct percussion

Direct percussion was the only method probably used by early hominids for hundreds of thousands of years. One direct percussion technique was the block-on-block. Here a large boulder was hurled to shatter a stone (fig. 40), and appropriate pieces were then used without further modification or were selected for further modification. The block-on-block technique also included a variation that provided better control in removing flakes. This variation was accomplished by swinging the core against an anvil (Crabtree 1972:34–35, 48). A more sophisticated use of direct percussion was the systematic removal of flakes by striking the edge of an implement (fig. 41). Although the direct percussion method required the minimum amount of strength, accuracy, uniformity, and predictability often were sacrificed.

Figure 40. The block-on-block technique of fracturing stone.

Figure 41. Percussion flaking.

The use of a punch as an intermediary instrument permitted greater accuracy, uniformity, and predictability. Stoneworkers sometimes used this method with a partner (Holmes 1919:296). However, I have seen no evidence that indirect percussion was used in Florida.

Indirect percussion

The striking platform is the surface area of the stone receiving the force necessary to detach a flake or blade (fig. 32).

Striking platforms

With an unprepared striking platform, a stoneworker simply used a follow-through motion, aimed at a convenient projection on the parent rock, and detached a flake with a minimum amount of effort but with a minimum of expected uniformity. During early time periods, or in areas where great quantities of raw materials were available, stoneworkers might break rock after rock, keeping for completion or for further modification only the rocks that happened to flake properly. Unprepared platforms tend to be large, and the bulb of force is usually salient (prominent), indicating that a tremendous (greater than necessary) force was exerted to detach the flake.

99

Stoneworking Technology

Striking platforms are said to be prepared when flakes have been removed from the core to isolate the platform or when the platform has been ground. A ground platform is nearly always seen on thinning flakes and blades and reflects the necessity to remove any irregularities that might interfere with accuracy, predictability, and uniformity of flake removal. Prepared platforms are an essential step in pressure flaking because, for example, when removing pressure blades the previous platform grinding ensures that the blade will detach more easily from the core (Crabtree 1980:personal communication).

Percussors

Without suitable flaking implements even the most skilled knapper would have difficulty in producing well-made stone tools. Hard hammer percussors made of stone, very often river-rounded cobbles, were widely used for the preliminary dressing of the chert material; but in Florida, where river cobbles did not exist, chert hammers were made by knocking off the edges of a large flake or core (fig. 25). Using a stone hammer for fine flaking was not very satisfactory because it tended to shatter the area at and near the striking platform. When subsequent reduction was attempted the "injured" stone simply could not be flaked predictably; in fact, it would fall apart. Shattering is particularly likely when a stone hammer is used on a tough heterogeneous material like Florida chert, whose flaking requires a great deal of force. Often a chert knapper can feel the shock of a hard hammer blow throughout the arm and shoulder. With obsidian, however, a small river pebble can be used for fairly fine flake removal by simply brushing the pebble across the edge of the obsidian at the appropriate angle.

Soft hammer percussors of antler, bone, or hardwood were desirable because they did not damage the chert inasmuch as the blow was absorbed by the material. The bulb of percussion that usually results from soft hammer flake detachment is diffused (flat), although an alternative explanation is offered by Bradley (1978:8–10). The length of a soft hammer permits it to be swung, adding extra force through the extension and making a better follow-

100

through motion possible. A stone hammer would need to be hafted to achieve the same results. Another advantage of the soft hammer is that it provides purchase; that is, it tends to adhere or hold fast to the object.

Flaking chert by pressure methods was probably the last major flintworking technique to be developed; it dates back at least to the Upper Paleolithic period in Europe, about 35,000 years ago.

Even though the principle of pressure flaking is essentially the same as with percussion, a tremendous difference must have existed in the mental set of the person who selected a pressure over a percussion method. Pressure flaking is a technique used for final retouching and for uniformity of flake dimension whereas percussion flaking employs an initial impact shaping technique. In the former method the area of impact or striking platform is always small because pressure flaking is used primarily to remove unwanted irregularities and to sharpen the edge without decreasing the overall size of the implement. In addition, we cannot ignore the possibility that pressure-flaked implements were aesthetically pleasing to their owner and were perhaps sometimes made for aesthetic rather than solely functional reasoning.

In pressure flaking a stoneworker places a small pointed flaker on the edge of the stone being fashioned and literally presses off the flake (fig. 42). This method requires maximum strength and provides maximum accuracy, uniformity, and predictability. This finishing method was more time consuming than percussion flaking.

A flaking crutch was a specialized tool for pressure flaking, evidence of which I have not observed in Florida. A chest crutch was used to provide added thrust to the point of impact so that large uniform blades could be removed as in the Mesoamerican polyhedral core tradition.

The pointed end of a deer tine seems to have been the most common tool for pressure flaking. It provided purchase and was

Pressure flaking

Pressure flaking with crutch

Pressure flakers

101

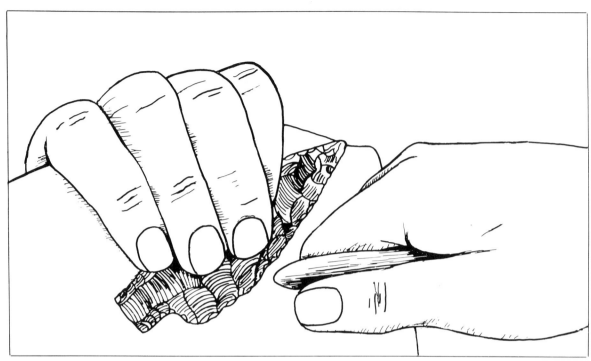

Figure 42. Pressure flaking.

dense enough to press off the flakes. Other materials, such as hafted teeth of certain animals, were also prized as flakers. John Smith says of the Indians of Virginia:

> To make the noch of his arrow hee hath the tooth of a Bever set in a sticke, wherewith he grateth it by degrees. His arrow head he quickly maketh with a little bone, which he ever weareth at his bracer (Swanton 1946:572).

Discussion

In addition to striking techniques, platform preparation, and flaking implements, a stoneworker had to vary the angle of the force to be applied, depending upon the type of flake to be removed. He also had to provide some kind of support (usually his knee) for the implement being flaked. Support is very important when a specimen is thin. In that case, flake removal becomes difficult due to inertia and lateral snap is more likely to occur if greater force is applied to overcome the inertia.

The native peoples of Florida did not utilize all of the stone chipping techniques that had been developed in other cultures. For instance, I have seen no indication that indirect percussion or pressure with a crutch was ever employed in Florida. Even the sophisticated blades associated with the Paleo Indian period and the rather anomalous blade production at the Newnan Lake site (8-A1-356) (Clausen 1964) could have been executed by direct percussion. With the possible exception of microliths (see chapter 2), Florida blades lack the precision of the polyhedral blade and core tradition of Mesoamerica. One can only speculate that the true blade technique is missing in Florida because (1) of the heterogeneity of the raw material, (2) there was no need for blades in the culture, (3) the people were unaware of the technique, or (4) blade making is a material-conserving method and there was no need to husband the plentiful stone resources.

Man is a practical mechanic, interested in producing a tool to perform a task (Mewhinney 1957).

Implement manufacturing

Introduction

In order to create a tangible object it is necessary to have a notion of how the finished object will look and how to proceed to accomplish the desired result. Any item of material culture is the product of an idea from the mind of a person and requires a plan to complete the contemplated. A similar creative progression is essential in stone tool manufacture, if only partially, even when a nodule is merely shattered and a piece suitable to perform the planned function is selected from the debitage. In interpreting the data he recovers, a cultural historian must reverse the maker's thought sequence: finished product ⇨ process of manufacture ⇨ idea in the mind of the maker. Not always does sufficient evidence exist to make this possible; explanations may be as varied as the number of scholars who analyze the material seeking to substantiate recognizable *patterns* of activity.

To distinguish between formal or future-use tools versus informal or convenience tools is pertinent. One does not use the same criteria to classify tools in these two separate major categories. Patterns are easier to determine among the more formal tools because their manufacture involved a complex combination of steps not accidentally repeatable. In other words, in fashioning a future-use tool, the flintknapper follows a preconceived trajectory of manufacturing techniques. The shape of the future-use tool is determined by the use to which it *will* be put. The shape of the convenience tool is often determined by the use to which it *was* put and might result from (1) its original size and shape, (2) the raw material from which it was made, (3) its duration and intensity of use, (4) whether its edge had been rejuvenated, or (5) the original intention of the toolmaker to use only the removed flakes rather than the recovered artifact itself. Thus, the "tool" that results is not the end product of a controlled trajectory of manufacturing techniques but results from fortuitous events. Put another way, toolmakers would tend to perfect and elaborate formal tools because those tools were used directly to perform a task (e.g., projectile points to kill animals), whereas they would use informal tools to perform tasks for which the unmodified implement happened to be suitable (e.g., to scrape and shape a spear shaft). For this reason, future-use tools may be classified on the basis of shape, but convenience tools should be classified on the basis of function because morphologically similar specimens may have functioned quite differently.

My conclusion concerning stone tool manufacture in early Florida is that when a flake with a steep angle (as for an adze) or a flake with a low angle (as for a knife) was needed, a native knapper had no difficulty in removing from a core a spall of the desired shape after judging the appropriate method of striking (amount of force, velocity, and angle) and selecting a suitable percussor. However, even though it is clear that early Florida people possessed stoneworking skills adequate of the manufacture of formal or future-use tools, lithic studies (including studies of informal or convenience tools) directed toward an understanding of flintworking techniques from the standpoint of the craftsman himself and the tasks his tools would perform increasingly will identify changes in techniques that very often signal changes in tasks and, therefore, changes in culture.

Florida projectile point manufacturing

I have recovered from the Senator Edwards Chipped Stone Workshop site (8-Mr-154) in Marion County, Florida, 2,050 Preceramic Archaic stemmed projectile points in various stages of completion. The specimens included 750 broken tips, 350 broken stemmed bases, 600 broken unstemmed bases, 250 unbroken preforms, and 94 complete projectile points. The study of these formal, future-use tools is here presented as an example of the explanation I have come up with in my efforts to substantiate patterns in Preceramic Archaic Florida manufacturing techniques.

The area directly under the cortex of Florida chert nodules appears to have been the most desirable flint source for projectile point manufacture. Many specimens broken in the early stages of manufacture retain cortex on the dorsal surface. Flake detachment could not proceed in a systematic way, as with polyhedral cores, because Florida chert nodules are too irregular and too fossiliferous; therefore, flakes were removed from any location on the nodules and in any direction (fig. 43).

Figure 43. Chert nodule with flake scars and flakes suitable for projectile point manufacture.

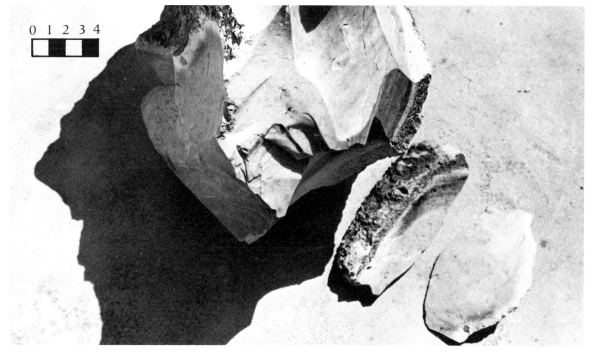

Stoneworking Technology

The large blade-like flakes characteristically have dorsal ridges, small striking platforms, small but salient bulbs, and triangular cross sections. The technique used to detach giant projectile point blades might have been the same technique used to detach classic blades during the Paleo Indian period. I can detach similar large blades by using a soft hammer with the weight concentrated in the head and directing the blow into the mass with a carry-through motion aiming at a small prepared striking platform.

The initial stage of stone tool production is the hardest to document for many reasons. If a flake of the desired size and shape was successfully detached from the core, it would obviously not be discarded but would be further refined as part of the process of manufacture. This flake would not break easily because of the flint mass and the method of detachment. Even if the flake did break as it was being removed from the core or shortly thereafter, it probably would have been used for another purpose since it would retain many desirable attributes: sharp cutting edge, flat ventral surface, and size large enough still to be converted into a serviceable tool. Such by-product items have been termed technologically dynamic, as opposed to technologically static, in an important observation by Katz and Katz (1975). It is important to note that the procedure stoneworkers used in the initial stage to remove flakes from a freshly struck blade may represent significant cultural differences. Of the four initial methods observed in Florida, two were present at the Edwards site and two other methods were seen on specimens from a nearby site (Bullen and Dolan 1959).

Method 1—Thinning the dorsal surface is the first step. The central ridge is reduced by removing flakes from each edge that extend beyond the midline. The only ventral flaking is a series of very short, stepped flakes near the edges. That flaking probably was done to remove the fragile feathering of the freshly struck flake, thus strengthening the edge and providing purchase for a percussor (fig. 44*a*). These specimens remain plano-convex, but as flaking proceeds the cross section becomes quite flattened (fig. 44*b*).

Method 2—The ventral surface is worked first, creating a rounding which did not exist originally. Since the dorsal ridge is left unflaked, the implement remains thick in cross section during much of the manufacturing process (fig. 44c).

Method 3—Flakes are removed from one edge, one face, and then from the opposite edge, opposite face (fig. 44d).

Method 4—Flakes are removed from both faces of one edge and then, presumably, from both faces of the other edge (fig. 44e).

Variations in these four methods of initial procedure must be significant, but whether they represent chronological, geographical, or traditional differences unfortunately cannot be determined at this time. Several Preceramic Archaic types, produced by methods 1 and 2, were collected at the Senator Edwards site, where the two methods were utilized about equally.

Symmetry and uniformity of flake removal were attempted in the earliest stages of manufacturing and maintained throughout all stages of projectile point manufacture. It was possible, therefore, to differentiate between specimens destined to become points and those destined to become other tools for which the attributes of uniformity and symmetry were not essential.

During manufacture uniform flake removal and symmetry were sought in three planes: (1) cross section—because at any phase in the manufacture process the symmetry might be lost, success with this plane was the hardest to accomplish, and it is possible to note throughout an attempt to maintain or reachieve symmetry (fig. 36a); (2) top view—rigidly maintained from the beginning of the manufacturing process (fig. 36b); (3) lateral view—rigidly maintained after being established at the beginning by removing the bulb and any curvature of the flake (fig. 36c).

Uniformity of flake removal should not be taken to mean that each flake is identical, only that flakes tend to be removed in the same direction and are of similar nature (e.g., broad and deep, long and narrow). One would not expect to find haphazard flake removal or flakes of very different sizes and shapes at any stage of manufacture (fig. 45). If symmetry and uniformity of flake removal are not present, it is safe to say the tool was probably not destined to be a projectile point.

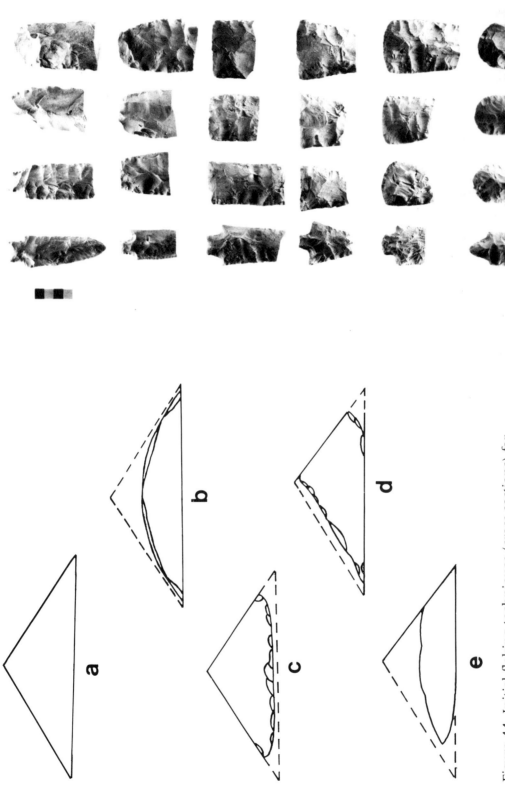

Figure 44. Initial flaking techniques (cross sections) for projectile point manufacture: (*a*) flake as removed from core, (*b*) dorsal surface has been reduced, (*c*) ventral surface has been reduced, (*d*) dorsal surface of one side and ventral surface of opposite side has been reduced, (*e*) dorsal and ventral surfaces of one side have been reduced.

Figure 45. Uniformity of flake removal in projectile point manufacture.

An exception to this uniformity would be a novice's attempt. Occasionally, specimens are encountered whose flaking is crude and whose symmetry is not maintained. These simply are poorly made points and cannot be classified as anything else. The number of poorly made specimens at the Senator Edwards site indicates the probability of the presence of novice stoneworkers. We would expect tutelage logically to have been conducted at a quarry work site. The fossiliferous nature of Florida chert might be another reason for the crudeness of manufacture of certain points. On unfinished broken points (fig. 35) a fossil nearly always appears at the snap.

Even if the broken specimen shows signs of use, it doesn't contradict our requirement of symmetry because a broken specimen might have been used to perform a nonanticipated task, sometimes many generations later (i.e., technologically dynamic). The recovery of heavily patinated specimens that have obviously been reflaked and ethnographic evidence (e.g., Gould et al. 1971:163) both support this contention.

Processual stages for all types present at the Senator Edwards site could not be documented. Some artifacts exhibit a stage reached during the manufacturing process prior to stemming and final shaping when both faces were extensively flaked. When examining such specimens the archaeologist is hard pressed to determine what the ultimate type was intended to be. It is quite possible that manufacturing techniques for all points could have been similar, differing only in the shaping of the stem; that is, nearly identical preforms might have been converted into different final forms.

The problem is compounded with the addition of the attempts of the novice toolmaker whose work cannot be expected to show the patterned, predictable techniques of an expert toolmaker. The novice's products, therefore, also fall outside of the expected processual stages. As nearly as can be determined at the Senator Edwards site, however, percussion flaking was employed throughout most of the projectile point manufacturing process. The first flakes removed are broad and deep, and an amazing amount of stone is removed with very little reduction in outer dimension. As thinning and shaping proceeds, flakes become long, shallow, and narrow. This may indicate that indirect percussion was used in these second stages, but I am inclined to believe it means a change in percussor or a change in force, velocity, or direction of the blow. Platforms were extensively ground in preparation for flake removal.

Pressure flaking was used only for final retouching, probably to remove irregularities and sharpen the edges. Pressure flaking seldom extends beyond the midline or exhibits the even, rippling effect seen on points such as the Eden and Scottsbluff points recovered in the western United States.

Nearly all flaking is at right angles to the lateral edges. There is little basal thinning except when necessary to shape the stem. Shaping of the stem occurred at different stages of manufacture depending upon the type of point being produced. At least two types recovered from the Senator Edwards site were stemmed while the ventral surface remained unflaked except for the stem area. In both of these cases, however, the dorsal surface had been reduced to such an extent that the cross section was quite flattened.

Heat treated projectile points were common at the Senator Edwards site. Observations were made on broken projectile point bases to determine at what stage of manufacture thermal alteration (see chapter 4) normally occurred and to determine the frequency of this practice at this site during the Florida Preceramic Archaic period. Specimens were included in the count only if it was certain they had been altered. In some cases left out, for instance, patina obscured evidence of heat treatment. Decisive evidence of heat treatment was found on 747 specimens, of which 495 were unstemmed and 252 were stemmed. Of the unstemmed bases only 65 had been heated while 430 had not. Of the broken stemmed bases 188 had been heated while 64 had not. Out of a sample of 94 unbroken projectile points from the Senator Edwards site, 63 were definitely heated, and 14 not. Heat treatment cannot be verified on 17 specimens but probably some of these had undergone heat alteration.

Although heating commonly took place fairly late in the manufacturing process, considerable variation is seen in the stage at which thermal treatment occurred, even within specific type groups. Stemming usually occurred after heating and preliminary thinning and shaping. After heating, points were reflaked completely by percussion, which removed the dull outer surface and imparted a vitreous luster to the entire implement. Pressure flaking occurred only as final retouching and usually did not obliterate flake scars produced previously by percussion.

Among 70,000 pieces of stone analyzed from the Senator Edwards site only 42 specimens can be classified as hammerstones of any kind. Taking this into account, it is probable that projectile point makers at the Edwards site worked with nonsurviving percussors made of dense bone or antler rather than of stone. The block-on-block technique could have been employed to break the large nodules, followed by finish flaking done with the nonsurviving soft hammers.

The small Florida deer, the largest antlered animal in Florida during the past 10,000 years, was approximately the same size during the Preceramic Archaic period as it is today. The antler of a large Florida deer probably would not exceed 4 cm in diameter. While this might be large enough to detach some small flakes by percussion, this lightweight antler would be more likely to rebound if used in early manufacturing stages against a large mass. On the other hand, deer antler tines would be quite suitable for pressure flaking. Deer tibiae and metapodials may have been utilized as flakers. The tubercles of anterior proximal tibiae as well as deer metapodials have been found at Florida archaeological sites and appear to be battered.

Another possible source of material for percussion is manatee rib, a very dense bone, fairly flat in cross section. Used as a flaking instrument its weight is concentrated in the head of the implement and can be directed at a very small striking platform. Recent flintworking experiments using seasoned manatee rib have produced excellent results. No ancient manatee bone, however, has been excavated at Preceramic sites in Florida—although cut and worked fossilized manatee bones, along with other fossilized bones and Paleo Indian and more recent projectile points, have been found in concentrated locations along the Chipola, Santa Fe, and Withlacoochee rivers. In addition, a number of shell midden sites have yielded manatee remains, and from ethnographic sources it is known that manatee was hunted in Florida (Cumbaa 1973). No organic remains of any kind have been preserved from the Senator Edwards site, and with the absence of hard hammerstones or large antlered animals I suggest that manatee rib may have provided a suitable flaking implement or percussor. Using manatee rib I can replicate the flakes recovered from the Senator Edwards site.

Summary

This investigation demonstrates that stone tool makers proceeded in a patterned, predictable, repetitive way. At each stage of projectile point manufacture, any one of several techniques might have been employed; that is, a similar product might result from any of various techniques. At the same time, different types might emerge from the use of similar techniques. It is not possible to determine the exact motor skills involved or to say precisely how a specimen was held while it was being flaked, but it is possible to suggest within a range the actual behavior and the idea in the mind of the maker while he was taking off flakes.

The study of projectile point manufacture described above was confined to specimens from a single site, the Senator Edwards Chipped Stone Workshop site, and to a single period, the Preceramic Archaic. Similar studies are needed for other areas, other periods, and other tool categories.

FOUR

Technical Analysis to Determine Age and Origin of Florida Chert Implements

Primitive craftsmen were as concerned with the properties of their raw materials as they were with the stylistic niceties of the finished item.

(Purdy 1976)

Early archaeological reports often were restricted to descriptions of artifacts. Eventually, time and geological relationships of specimens were established, based principally upon those descriptions. Later, speculation on the use of artifacts was offered. More recent research has been directed toward techniques of manufacture. The next logical step has been to determine the properties of the raw materials selected by prehistoric peoples in order to gain a greater insight into their technological achievements. In order for us to do this, it is first necessary to properly identify the origin and age of prehistoric remains.

A variety of instrumental techniques have been developed in the physical sciences that can be used to help answer archaeological questions. The methods I have been using to analyze Florida cherts were chosen because of their potential to provide the most significant results and because major equipment and qualified, cooperative personnel have been available. Basic research has questioned the

Introduction

113

source and quality of stone materials, changes brought about by
weathering and heating, and the antiquity of man in Florida and the
Western Hemisphere. Information derived from these analyses has
been stored in a readily available data bank and can be used both
now and in the future to answer questions about Florida cherts (see
fig. 18).

Two statements need to be made about the use of instrumental
analyses. First, the methods are often complex, time-consuming,
expensive, and involve the use of equipment that archaeologists are
not trained to operate. While initial results from a limited sample
may be exciting to the archaeologist, to demonstrate objectively what
those results represent requires many a valid generalization, many
hours of preparation, and access to specialized equipment, trained
personnel, and money. The archaeologist needs to be certain that the
information received from an experiment is going to be important
enough to justify its being done, particularly if the artifact will be
destroyed by the analytic technique.

Second, assuming that a thorough study has been concluded, the
interpretation of the data becomes only one part of the answer
sought. For example, even radiocarbon dates are considered valid
only when they agree with other available information.
Archaeologists today, endeavoring to be more scientific than their
predecessors, sometime believe that an instrumental analysis
substitutes for other types of systematic observations. This
occasionally appears to be the case with the ubiquitous present-day
application of elaborate statistical methods. Sophisticated statistical
and computer analysis may not always be necessary, especially if
data-gathering and the distribution of the raw data are equally
conclusive. At any rate, statistical methods should be used as only
part of any study.

Primarily because of time, cost, equipment, and technical assistance
requirements, no analyses of Florida chert using the methods
described in this chapter have yet been completed; but, a
description of the methods, their potential, and the preliminary

findings may be of interest to individuals seeking more complete
information about artifact remains.

Flint materials are usually composed of 70–99 percent silica with
other constituents present as major or minor trace elements. A study
of the trace element composition of Florida cherts can provide much
information about primitive raw material selection, about prehistoric
events such as migrations, and about trade routes. Establishment of
the normal variations for trace elements in naturally occurring
peninsular Florida cherts can serve as a reference standard with
which to compare element composition of particular stone artifacts.
Based on this comparison certain tests can be made of archaeological
hypotheses.

(1) People in Florida during the Paleo Indian period were not full-
time residents—a comparison of trace elements in the points from
this period with the standard for peninsular Florida would detect the
presence of out-of-state cherts.

(2) There was preferential selection of chert materials by prehistoric
stoneworkers because some easily accessible outcrops were ignored
while others were heavily exploited—if projectile points show less
variation in quantities of trace elements than does the available
supply of raw material, some kind of selection, perhaps for quality,
must have been practiced.

(3) When extensive exploitation of chert sources in the central
highlands of Florida ceased about 5,000 years ago, following
population shifts, raw material for projectile points were then
obtained through trade from only a few locations—a comparison with
the trace element standards would identify the locations as well as
confirm the hypothesis.

(4) Changes in chemical composition that occur with weathering
may be correlated with the rate of weathering, thus providing a way
of assigning at least relative dates to archaeological assemblages—
these changes can be detected by comparison with the standards.

Several techniques having differing degrees of sensitivity can be used to identify and quantify trace element composition. Element profiles of Florida cherts have been compiled using particle induced X-ray emission analysis (PIXE analysis) (Mock 1978) and neutron activation analysis (NAA) (Purdy and Roessler n.d.), but larger numbers of samples must be tested before the information can serve as a standard to which other stone material can be compared.

Particle induced X-ray emission (PIXE) analysis

Characteristic X rays excited by electrons and by other X rays have long been used for elemental analysis. PIXE analysis is an improvement over classical X-ray fluorescence techniques because it uses more sensitive X-ray detectors.

Procedure

Excitation of the samples occurs through bombardment by charged particles accelerated to several megavolts. Charged particles produced in the ion source of an accelerator are accelerated to the appropriate energy and focused on the sample to be analyzed. A spectrum of X rays characteristic of the elements present in the sample is produced during the bombardment and detected by an X-ray detector using the semiconductor Si(Li). It is the remarkable increase in sensitivity and resolution of these detectors, along with the extremely large number of X rays produced during bombardment, that makes detection of 0.1 to 1.0 routine. These sensitivities can generally be achieved in approximately 15 minutes using as little as 100 μg of material. The capacity of the Si(Li) detector is such that one can easily identify, through their characteristic X rays, consecutive elements in the periodic table as low as $z>11$ (sodium). Another advantage of PIXE analysis stems from the fact that the generated spectrum will permit the simultaneous determination of all trace elements. The same run will also give ample information on elements which are below the detection limits of other methods. Quantitative determination is generally achieved by calibration of the system with standard materials. The complete analytic equipment necessary for this type of research is available on the University of Florida campus, including a 4 MeV Van de Graaff accelerator. For a more complete description of the method see Mock (1978).

116

Chert specimens were collected from a number of locations in the portion of the Florida peninsula where chert outcrops are known to exist or where deposits lie close to the surface. The sites were selected for their wide geographic distribution, for their abundance of the chert, and because of indications of exploitation by primitive peoples. Two additional samples were tested, one from the Florida Panhandle and the other from Kentucky (Dover Flint). Each sample represented an individual rock, from which a portion was chipped, cleaned of all weathering, and ground up by a steel ball mill into a fine powder. After the chert powder passed through a 0.005 mm sieve, it was pressed into a thick target pellet using a steel die. The finished target pellet measured 2 cm in diameter and was approximately 0.25 cm thick. It was then mounted in an aluminum target frame, which exposed one face of the pellet to the beam. (Five targets can be mounted on the target ladder and placed in the target chamber. This arrangement allows five consecutive samples to be studied without the necessity of breaking the vacuum inside the target chamber to change samples.) The grinding homogenizes small-scale variations within the intact specimen, and it allows the creation of a uniform surface texture in the pellet for best exposure to the particle beam. This is important in assuring the reproducibility of the results (Mock 1978:18–19).

As characterized by PIXE analysis, Florida cherts contain aluminum, silicon, potassium, calcium, titanium, iron, copper, zinc, rubidium, strontium, zirconium, and lead in appreciable amounts (fig. 46). Vanadium and chromium appear in many of the samples, while manganese and nickel appear in only a few. In addition to the elements cited in tables 3 and 4, one sample contains 480 parts per million of barium. Tin is present in very small quantities in eight samples. The Kentucky sample conains yttrium, as does the specimen from the Panhandle, which also contains molybdenum and ruthenium. Two samples are quite different from the other peninsular cherts: one is almost devoid of trace elements—a fact that

PIXE analysis of Florida chert

117

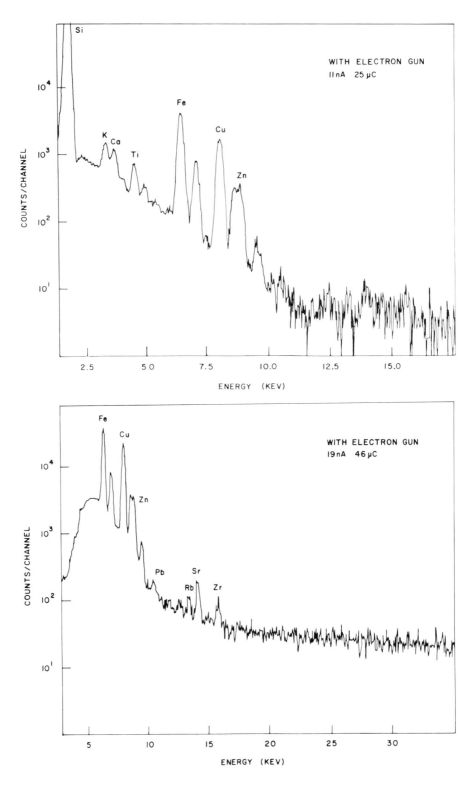

Figure 46. Typical chert spectra obtained through bombardment by 2.0 MeV protons and 3.0 MeV protons.

Table 3
Element concentrations (PPM) using 2.0 MeV protons

Sample	Potassium	Calcium	Titanium	Vanadium	Chromium	Manganese	Iron	Nickel	Copper	Zinc
S1	904±124	503±69	174±24	21.9±4.2	–	–	2571±352	–	44.2±6.1	–
S2	1021±140	531±73	184±25	34.9±5.2	7.3±2.0	–	1895±260	–	359±49	81±11
S3 Santa Fe R.	628±87	331±45	105±14	10.4±2.6	–	–	490±67	12.2±2.1	678±93	135±19
S4	728±100	359±49	116±16	12.6±2.6	–	–	1031±141	–	695±95	141±19
S5	741±102	384±53	117±24	74±11	–	58.1±8.0	9670±1320	–	345±47	71±10
S6	143±26	59.0±8.3	–	–	–	–	608±83	–	7.1±1.4	–
S7	796±109	249±34	152±21	43.9±6.3	9.7±2.4	–	1925±264	–	961±132	203±28
S8 Aucilla R.	711±98	304±42	146±20	27.0±4.5	8.0±2.4	–	2643±362	–	530±73	104±14
S9	927±127	311±43	185±25	25.9±4.3	–	–	2041±280	–	312±43	49.8±7.5
S10	918±126	399±55	187±26	30.6±4.6	8.0±2.2	–	3063±420	–	74±10	12.5±2.5
S11	723±100	33200±4550	105±14	21.3±4.1	30.6±5.0	–	406±56	–	630±86	133±18
S12 CCA site	142±26	598±82	43.1±7.0	–	123±17	–	10842±1480	–	747±10	150±21
S13	819±112	475±65	186±26	33.0±5.0	12.9±2.8	–	7028±963	–	360±49	63.3±8.8
S14	688±94	419±57	201±28	37.6±5.7	19.1±4.0	–	11204±1530	–	414±57	112±15
S15 Zephyrhills	825±113	287±39	258±35	95±13	–	4.9±2.0	600±82	–	806±110	188±25
S16 Kentucky	1818±249	2421±330	399±55	28.0±5.0	–	151±21	2421±332	6.3±1.7	522±72	138±19
S17 Panhandle	166±27	191±26	63±10	–	144±20	11.2±2.4	8512±1166	–	120±16	494±68

Table 4
Element concentrations (PPM) using 3.0 MeV protons

Sample		Rubidium	Strontium	Zirconium	Lead
S1		6.97±1.20	10.1±1.8	6.20±1.25	11.3±1.8
S2		6.62±0.92	9.91±1.78	8.93±1.70	6.77±1.2
S3	Santa Fe R.	8.90±1.48	9.29±1.56	12.1±2.1	32.2±4.6
S4		7.48±1.32	19.6±2.9	7.56±1.64	11.0±1.9
S5		8.77±1.63	16.9±2.5	16.2±2.6	19.7±3.0
S6		–	–	–	6.81±1.6
S7		8.34±1.39	6.40±1.27	11.9±2.1	11.1±2.0
S8	Aucilla R.	4.43±0.85	6.14±1.30	3.08±1.43	11.1±2.1
S9		12.6±1.9	7.86±1.38	10.1±1.9	11.6±2.1
S10		9.95±1.73	7.16±1.45	9.00±1.79	15.7±2.5
S11		7.89±1.40	16.6±2.5	12.2±2.3	21.7±3.3
S12		7.05±1.42	5.37±1.23	–	–
S13	CCA Site	8.54±1.51	4.81±1.09	9.56±1.81	9.90±1.8
S14		7.42±1.60	8.68±1.67	15.4±2.7	28.8±4.4
S15	Zephyrhills	6.64±1.55	12.1±2.0	9.80±1.94	26.2±3.7
S16	Kentucky	12.0±2.0	39.5±5.4	17.0±2.8	8.73±1.7
S17	Panhandle	9.31±1.62	50.4±6.9	67.2±9.3	–

might be explained by extreme weathering of the sample; another has a high concentration of calcium—a fact that might be accounted for if replacement of calcium carbonate by silica were incomplete.

The copper-to-zinc ratio seems to remain fairly constant for the peninsular specimens, and the potassium-to-calcium ratio appears to follow a subregional grouping. The relevance of these statistical trends can only be proven by more exhaustive studies involving larger numbers of chert samples.

By remeasuring three of the pellets it was determined that the results are reproducible with an average error of 15–20 percent (Mock 1978:28–35).

Neutron activation analysis (NAA)

Activation analysis can be defined as chemical analysis by means of induced radioactivity to make use of nuclear reactions resulting in radioactive species of atoms, whose disintegration characteristics are subsequently determined and used as a basis for identifying the elements originally present in the sample. The most commonly used primary particles which cause these reactions are thermal neutrons. In valuable ways activation analysis supplements conventional analytical techniques and permits analysis without chemical manipulation, which is sometimes impractical or impossible. Neutron activation analysis is a nondestructive, highly sensitive technique (0.1 to 10 ppb at 10 percent precision). The theory behind activation analysis is based on the formation of different radioactive nuclides as a result of reactions between nuclear particles and the various isotopes of the elements being measured. Each isotope is transformed into a different isotope of either the same or of a different element. There are many nuclear reactions which, in principle, can be utilized for this diagnostic purpose. An appropriate counter is used to measure the radioactivity in an irradiated sample.

Neutron activation analysis can be either qualitative or quantitative. Qualitatively it is used to detect elements whose presence is unsuspected and to indicate whether enough of a given element is present to make feasible a quantitative analysis. In a quantitative analysis, the test sample and a standard sample containing a known concentration of the element to be determined are both irradiated simultaneously and are processed in the same manner. The amounts of radioactivity produced in the standard and in the test sample are then compared and the concentration of the element in the test sample calculated.

Procedure

At the University of Florida the emphasis has been on direct instrumental analysis of many materials, including chert, using selected irradiation regimes, the appropriate gamma spectrometry system, and computer routines that resolve specta, identify peaks, calculate activities, and quantify the elements originally present. The University of Florida has complete facilities for thermal neutron activation of samples, analysis of activated samples, and computation of results. These facilities include (1) a training reactor licensed to operate up to 100 kW(th) producing a thermal neutron flux of 4×10^{12} n/cm^2-sec in the center vertical port, (2) a computer-based gamma spectrometer analysis system consisting of an 80 cm^3 lithium-drifted germanium [Ge(Li)] diode coupled to a computer-based 4096 multichannel analyzer (MCA), (3) a low energy photon spectrometer system that has the advantage of minimizing interference of higher energy gamma rays when performing analysis of samples having mixed compositions, and (4) a complete radiochemistry laboratory.

NAA of Florida
chert

Using the same samples as those used for PIXE analysis, NAA identified scandium, chromium, iron, cobalt, zinc, cesium, iridium, platinum, gold, bromium, antimony, barium, lanthanum, and selenium. There was very close agreement in measurements of element concentrations obtained with PIXE and those obtained with NAA (see tables 3 and 4). A number of elements were detected by NAA that could not be detected with PIXE and vice versa.

The application of both methods is valuable as a mutual check and because a broader spectrum of elements is revealed by utilizing both PIXE and NAA. Expanded investigations using larger samples are necessary before a complete identification of Florida cherts can be obtained. A more complete discussion of the results of these studies is in preparation (Purdy and Roessler).

Thermal
alteration

The application of heat to flint materials provided an advantage to primitive man in his production of certain chipped stone implements (Crabtree and Butler 1964; Bordes 1969*b*). Until recently little was known about the technique or about what changes occurred in the rock material when it was heated. Extensive as well as intensive experiments were conducted to determine if alteration occurs when Florida cherts are heated, at what temperature alteration occurs, and what procedure must be followed in order to effect the most desirable change (Purdy and Brooks 1971; Purdy 1974, 1975*b*).

The critical temperature needed to alter Florida cherts is about 350°C. A color change takes place between 240°C and 260°C if minute amounts of iron are present. The color change is not synchronous with the significant vitreous change that occurs at 350°C. The scanning electron microscope illustrates the change that occurs when cherts are heated (fig. 47). The fractured surface of

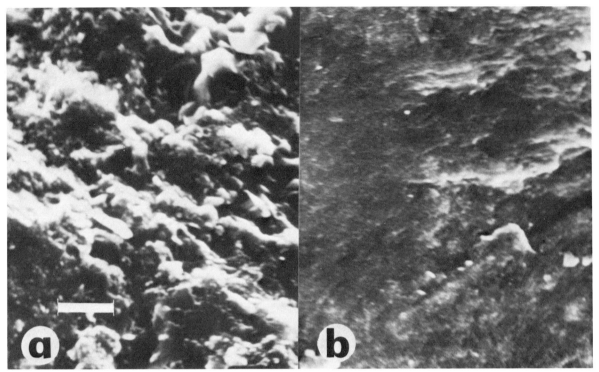

Figure 47. Scanning electron microscope photomicrograph showing differences in fracture patterns of heated and unheated Florida cherts.

unheated materials shows individual microcrystals resembling bread crumbs, whereas a surface fractured after the sample was heated is extremely smooth. In the heated samples fractures pass through the cryptocrystals rather than around the crystals as in unheated samples. The individual grains of the mineral quartz are held more firmly together in the heated specimen than in the unheated specimen. Minute amounts of impurities, or compounds of the elements making up the impurities, in the intercrystalline spaces of the chert are probably acting as fluxes to fuse a thin surface film of microcrystals. This is called eutectic development and it explains why alteration occurs at 350°C instead of between 1400°C and 1700°C, the temperature necessary to transform microcrystalline quartz structures to a noncrystalline form. Binding of the microcrystals results in a more uniform material with the ability to fracture like glass rather than like rock. After alteration has taken place, flakes tend to feather out rather than step off.

123

Technical Analysis

The results of compressive strength tests showed that unheated chert
controls withstood forces 40 percent greater than heated chert samples
that had been removed immediately from the hot oven. On the other
hand, chert samples that had been allowed to cool in the oven
withstood forces 25 percent greater than the unheated controls. Tensile
strength tests on points demonstrated that unheated controls withstood
forces 45 percent greater than heated chert samples that had been
allowed to cool slowly before removal from the oven. An additional
loss of strength, as much as 25 percent, occurred when the materials
were removed immediately from the hot oven at the termination of the
testing period or when the samples were exposed to temperatures
greater than those necessary to effect change. A discrepancy seems to
exist if a comparison is made between results obtained from
compressive strength tests and those from tensile strength tests. Under
compressive strength testing, when samples were allowed to cool in
the oven, they resisted failure longer than unheated controls. The
results of tests of tensile strength, on the other hand, revealed a
significant reduction in the time and load necessary to cause failure in
heated samples, regardless of whether they were removed from the
oven while hot or allowed to cool in the oven. However, this seeming
contradiction is easily explained. Binding of the microcrystals when
rock is heated adds compressive strength through cohesion. The
increase in uniformity that increases strength under compression is the
very factor that decreases point tensile strength. The individual
microcrystals are bound more firmly together; therefore, when a flaw
exists failure takes place more readily because the specimen responds
more like glass than like a rock aggregate. There is a 60 percent
reduction in the granular surface area of heated chert due to the
reduction of intergranular pore radii.

The changes that take place with thermal alteration produce a
structural and a compositional alteration. The change is gradual rather
than abrupt. If the sample is heated slowly to 350°C, kept at this
temperature for a sustained period, and then allowed to cool in

the oven, it develops the vitreous luster (seen with subsequent flaking) which appears to be the most significant visible characteristic of thermally altered Florida chert.

Our research refuted the mythical supposition that stone flaking was done with dripping water. Attempts to chip by dripping cold water on hot chert resulted in merely a crazing of the material (fig. 39). Any attempts to flake the material caused it to crumble— predictable fracture was impossible.

In conclusion, evidence indicates that primitive stoneworkers altered lithic raw material by slowly heating it to critical temperatures for sustained periods and allowing it to cool gradually. Alteration takes place when the melting point of the impurities within the intercrystalline spaces is reached. Thus, the microcrystals of quartz are fitted closer together when materials other than quartz are present to serve as fluxes. After thermal alteration, crystal boundaries no longer interfere with the removal of flakes. The material becomes easier to flake and has a sharper edge. Prehistoric peoples were probably well aware of the advantages this practice conferred in the manufacture of chipped stone implements, particularly those needing symmetry and balance, such as projectile points.

Because the use of fire and the use of stone were two of the earliest and most important items in the tool inventory it was inevitable that early people gradually acquired an intimate knowledge of their attributes. Prior to written records, however, there is little to imply how exact a worker had to be in order to accomplish certain tasks. The investigation of thermal alteration has demonstrated that primitive people needed to be very precise in their utilization of fire in order to alter lithic materials. It appears, also, that this precision differed from region to region and depended upon the type of flint available. In Florida, people were subjecting lithic raw materials to heat at least by the Early Archaic period, about 8,500 years ago (for discussions of historic observations of thermal alteration see Purdy 1971*b* and Hester 1972).

Technical Analysis

Thermoluminescent (TL) analysis

The principle of thermoluminescence is based on the fact that when certain materials are subjected to ionizing radiation, a fraction of the energy absorbed is stored in fairly stable electron arrangements which can later be measured as visible light if the material is heated.

Instrumentation for determining the amount of thermoluminescence was developed in the field of radiological health to measure X rays (Cameron et al. 1968). The technique has a potential at least as great as radiocarbon analysis for detecting the age of certain artifacts (Michael and Ralph 1971; Michels 1973; Tite 1972). Tools made from Florida chert having luminescent properties and having been subjected to heat as part of their manufacturing process are appropriate objects for thermoluminescent analysis. The energy traps in the chert tools were emptied (zeroed) when the chert was heated. The stone began storing energy again at a constant rate; therefore, it is possible to date the time of ancient heating by measuring the amount of light emitted when the specimen is subjected to heat the second time under laboratory conditions.

Thermoluminescent analysis can (1) date stone remains directly, (2) verify the reliability of radiocarbon dates, (3) date inorganic remains when carbon-containing materials are not present, and (4) reduce the dependence on typological comparison for chronological assignment of artifactual remains.

Procedure

The procedure for dating an artifact by thermoluminescence involves:

(1) Measurement of the amount of radioactivity present in the artifact and the environment so that the radiation dose to the sample can be estimated. The procedure identifies and quantifies radioactive elements to determine radiation dose in rads per time unit (d).

(2) Measurement of the natural TL (Gn) of stone tools to be dated. The sample is heated to release the stored energy. The visible light is accurately measured by a TL reader and recorded digitally.

(3) Exposure of the same samples to an "artificial" dose of radiation (D). A B^- emitter such as ^{90}Sr is used to simulate the

126

natural radioactivity to which the sample has been exposed since it was first heated by ancient toolmakers. This step determines the susceptibility of the material to irradiation. The thermoluminescence produced by the artificial exposure, (Ga), is then measured. The age, (T), of the sample is calculated by:

$$T = \frac{Gn}{Ga} \times \frac{D}{d}.$$

For a more complete discussion of the procedures and problems associated with thermoluminescent dating see Zimmerman (1978).

At the University of Florida, scientists in the Nuclear Engineering Department, the Material Sciences and Engineering Department, and the Geology Department are cooperating with me to date by thermoluminescence prehistoric stone implements that have been intentionally or accidentally heat altered. Thermoluminescent equipment has been purchased and is in operation in the Department of Geology.

Material Engineering scientists have developed techniques and kinetic equations for predicting the extent of weathering during the expected lifetime of a material. Similar analyses can be used to estimate the age of artifacts by measuring the extent of weathering.

Weathering studies

Reactions that occur between alkali–alkaline earth–silica materials (Florida cherts) and aqueous environments are well characterized (Clark et al. 1978). The interaction of these materials with their surroundings results in two general types of weathering (Clark et al. 1977): (1) Static weathering results when silicate materials are exposed to highly alkaline environments (>pH 9) (Clark, Acree, el al., 1976; Clark, Dilmore, et al. 1976). The Si-O-Si bonds that form the structural network of silicate materials are destroyed and total dissolution ensues. A typical example of this type of weathering occurs when the artifact is exposed to a standing pool of water over a long period of time. (2) Dynamic weathering occurs when the pH of the environment is maintained relatively neutral or even slightly acidic ($\leqslant$pH 7). The Si-O-Si bonds are unaffected and the primary reaction mechanism under these conditions is selective leaching of the alkali ions (Na^+, K^{++}, Li^{+++}) or of the transition metal ions from the material. A typical example of this would be the exposure of the artifact to a well-drained matrix of clay and sand. The equations for these two reactions are shown below.

Total dissolution or static weathering (1)

$$
\underset{\text{(material)}}{\overset{\displaystyle O \qquad O}{O-\overset{|}{\underset{|}{Si}}-O-\overset{|}{\underset{|}{Si}}-O}} \quad + \quad \underset{\text{+ (solution)}}{4\,OH^-} \quad \Rightarrow \quad \underset{\text{(solution)}}{\overset{\displaystyle HO}{HO-\overset{|}{\underset{|}{Si}}-OH}} \quad + \quad \underset{\text{(solution)}}{\overset{\displaystyle O^-}{^-O-\overset{|}{\underset{|}{Si}}-O^-}}
$$

Selective leaching or dynamic weathering (2)

$$
\underset{\text{(material)}}{\overset{\displaystyle O}{O-\overset{|}{\underset{|}{Si}}-O=Na}} \quad + \quad \underset{\text{+ (solution)}}{H^+} \quad \Rightarrow \quad \underset{\text{(material)}}{\overset{\displaystyle O}{O-\overset{|}{\underset{|}{Si}}-OH}} \quad + \quad \underset{\text{(solution)}}{Na^+}
$$

The effects of weathering are manifested by an alteration in two parameters (Sanders et al. 1972): surface roughness and surface composition. Surface roughness is a direct result of total dissolution or static weathering. Surface composition changes, which occur over a finite depth within the surface, are due primarily to dynamic weathering or patina formation. Figure 48 illustrates schematically the surface changes associated with both static and dynamic weathering.

128

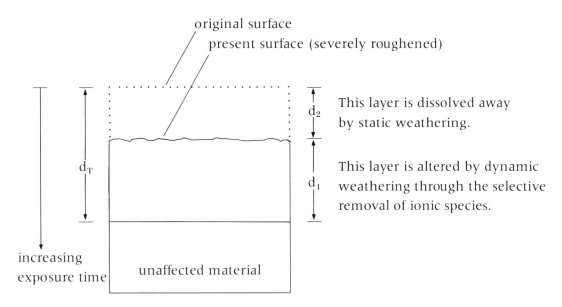

Figure 48. Schematic illustrating surface changes associated with chert weathering.

Both the extent of the surface roughening and the thickness of the selectively leached layer are dependent on the duration of exposure. The kinetics equation that relates the exposure time to the extent of surface roughening (static weathering) and the thickness of the selectively leached layer (dynamic weathering) follows:

$$d_T = \qquad d_1 \qquad + \qquad d_2 \qquad (3)$$

$$d_T = \qquad \underset{\substack{\text{dynamic} \\ \text{weathering}}}{K_1 \sqrt{t}} \qquad + \qquad \underset{\substack{\text{static} \\ \text{weathering}}}{K_2\, t} \qquad (3')$$

where:

d_T = total thickness of the affected surface
K_1, K_2 = experimentally determined reaction rate constants
t = duration of exposure (can be considered age of artifact)
d_1 = thickness of surface affected by dynamic weathering
d_2 = thickness of surface affected by static weathering.

Technical Analysis

The extent of dynamic weathering (d_1) and static weathering (d_2) can be measured using electron microprobe analysis (EMP) (Clark et al. 1975), and infrared reflection spectroscopy (IRRS) (Sanders et al. 1972).

Scientific weathering analyses

Electron microprobe analysis along with auger electron spectroscopy can be used to generate depth compositional profiles by evaluating compositional changes that occur both on and within the chert surface. Argon–ion milling (IM) measures the exact depth of compositional change by removing atomic layers of surface material. Figures 49 and 50 illustrate a profile for the major constituent, silica, and the major trace impurities, iron and aluminum, from a sample of patinated Florida chert. This sample was recovered 80–90 cm below the surface in a sandy clay horizon at the CCA site, 8-Mr-154, Marion County, Florida. Four distinctive layers can be seen: patina, interface, dark-colored area, and fresh or bulk material. The concentration of silica is slightly higher in the patinated layer (600 μm thick)

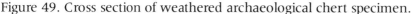

Figure 49. Cross section of weathered archaeological chert specimen.

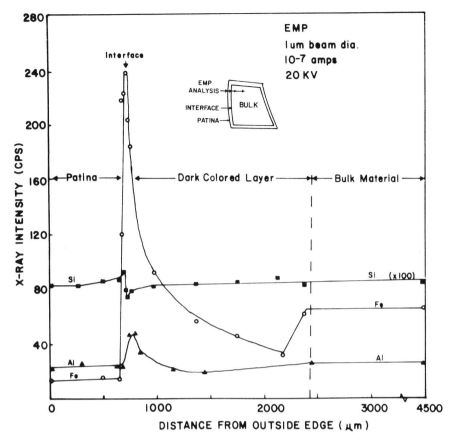

Figure 50. Depth compositional profile of specimen pictured in figure 49.

than in the fresh material, while the concentration of iron is lower
by a factor of 5. The aluminum concentration is approximately the
same in both the patinated and fresh material. Large alterations in the
concentration of all three elements occur at the interface (110 μm
thick). The concentrations of both iron and aluminum are much larger,
while the concentration of silica is smaller, in comparison to the fresh
material. In the dark-colored region adjacent to the interface, there is a
gentle decrease in both iron and aluminum concentrations. In this
region, the concentrations of these two elements is less than in the
fresh material. The concentrations for silica, iron, and aluminum reach
constant values at approximately 2,400 μm (2.4 mm) within the
material and maintain these values through the center of the
specimen.

131

Technical Analysis

What environmental storage factors are responsible for the evolution of the depth compositional profiles? This question may be answered in part by evaluating the profiles of a freshly fractured surface (unweathered) and the same surfaces exposed to controlled environments. These depth compositional profiles are shown in figure 51. The concentrations of silica, iron, and aluminum do not vary as a function of depth into the freshly fractured surface. However, when this same specimen is exposed to an aqueous environment (pH 3.5) for 500 hours at 100°C (i.e., accelerated weathering), significant alterations in the surface chemistry occur to a depth of <1 μm. These variations could not be detected with the EMP since the spatial resolution of this instrument is ~2 μm. Much longer laboratory exposure times are required before the EMP can be sensitive to chemical changes occurring near the surface. However, auger electron spectroscopy coupled with Argon–ion milling revealed that iron had been leached to a depth of at least 200 Å (0.02 μm) in the 500 hours/100°C weathered specimen. AES samples depths only 10–50 Å within the

Figure 51. Depth compositional profile of an artificially weathered chert specimen.

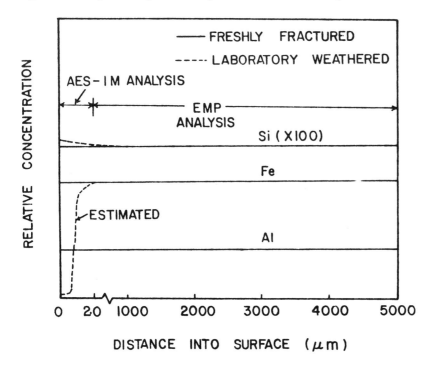

surface (Clark et al. 1978). The AES-IM technique is useful for monitoring compositional changes that occur from $0-2$ μm within the surface while EMP is useful for depths >2 μm. The joint use of these two techniques provide compositional information over the entire depth of reaction for both laboratory and field-weathered specimens.

Weathering reactions in chert are thought to be diffusion controlled. The following reaction mechanism is proposed. During exposure, hydrogen ions from the solution exchange with iron ions from the surface of the sample. This results in the development of a silica-rich (iron-depleted) surface that increases in thickness with time. Furthermore, the excess iron present at the interface suggests that the rate of the ion exchange (rate of patina growth) is controlled by the rate of iron diffusion through the patina. Thus, under special conditions, the thickness of the patina may be used as an age indicator.

How can the depth compositional profile be used as an indication of age of an artifact? As indicated in equation 3, the weathering process manifested in the form of a patina involves a time factor. By rearranging equation 3 and artifically weathering chert specimens in the laboratory under controlled conditions, the reaction rate constant (K) can be determined.

$$K = \frac{d}{\sqrt{t}}. \qquad (4)$$

Once the reaction rate constant is known, the age of the artifact may be calculated using:

$$t = \left(\frac{d}{K}\right)^2. \qquad (5)$$

If we can assume that the Indians used fresh material for manufacturing their tools, then the thickness (d) of the patina should provide an indication of the age of the tool. The thickness of the patina can be accurately determined using the EMP, as demonstrated in figure 50. An important question, as yet undetermined, is how sensitive K is to environmental temperature and how that affects the calculation of the age of the artifact. This question cannot be answered until K is accurately evaluated as a function of temperature. This work, taking 25°C as a norm, is presently in process in the Material Sciences and Engineering Department at the University of Florida.

One final topic that requires discussion is the role of the aluminum in the weathering of Florida chert. It is a well-established fact that Al_2O_3 retards weathering in high-silica materials. In fact, small aluminum additions in silicate glass melts are common practice in the glass industry (Clark et al. 1978). Likewise, for the Florida cherts, it appears that aluminum plays an important role in the weathering process. Although aluminum is not leached from the surface, it does concentrate at the interface, as shown in figure 50. Thus, although aluminum does not enter into the ion exchange reactions, it may promote or retard the iron-hydrogen (Fe-H) exchange reaction. A fuller understanding of the behavior of aluminum during weathering may provide an additional technique for estimating the age of lithic artifacts.

Infrared Reflection Spectroscopy (IRRS)

Infrared reflection spectroscopy (IRRS) has been used for several years to monitor reactions and associated structural alterations that occur during weathering of silicate glasses (Clark et al. 1977; Hench and Clark 1978; Sanders et al. 1972). IRRS is rapid, inexpensive, and nondestructive and provides both structural and chemical information about material surfaces. IRRS is presently being examined in the Material Sciences and Engineering Department by David E. Clark as a potential technique for evaluating weathered chert. Specimens exhibiting each type of weathering were snapped to expose the cross section as shown in figure 52. IRRS spectra of the outer surface are presented in figure 53 for the three specimens. The spectra of vitreous silica is also shown in this figure, to illustrate its similarity to the chert specimens and for the purpose of calibration. In this figure, the amplitude (intensity) of the reflected infrared radiation (referenced to a mirror) is plotted as a function of incident radiation wavenumber (wavelength). Major spectral changes occur between 1300 cm^{-1} to 1000 cm^{-1}. The major reflection peaks in this region are due to the silicate symmetrical stretch vibrations (S) in the silica tetrahedral structure. During weathering, the wavenumber position and the amplitude of these peaks may change, due to selective leaching of impurities or network breakdown from the chert surface. The dark brown specimen retrieved from level 4, which shows no evidence of weathering, reflects 76 percent of the incident 1190 cm^{-1} radiation. The gray material from level 2 reflects 57 percent; and the extremely weathered specimen from level 9 reflects only 23 percent of the 1190 cm^{-1} radiation. Thus, the IRRS spectra are definitely influenced by the extent of weathering on the chert surface. Chert specimens are presently being artificially weathered in controlled environments. The infrared reflection data obtained from these specimens should allow us to quantitatively establish the relationship between extent of weathering and IRRS peak behavior (Clark and Purdy 1979a, 1979b; Purdy and Clark 1979).

The primary objective, using EMP, AES, IM, and IRRS techniques is to develop a method to date Florida chert artifacts by evaluating the surface chemical and structural changes that accompany weathering. Since very little organic material has been preserved in Florida that can be used for radiocarbon dating, the development of this method is very important. The research procedure is as follows:

(1) Evaluate the surface alterations that have occurred on field specimens subjected to natural weathering.

(2) Evaluate surface changes that occur on fresh specimens (i.e., unweathered) of similar materials during artificially controlled laboratory weathering.

(3) Reduce the data obtained in the second step to a formula.

At present, correlation between exposure time and surface properties is being experimentally determined at the University of Florida.

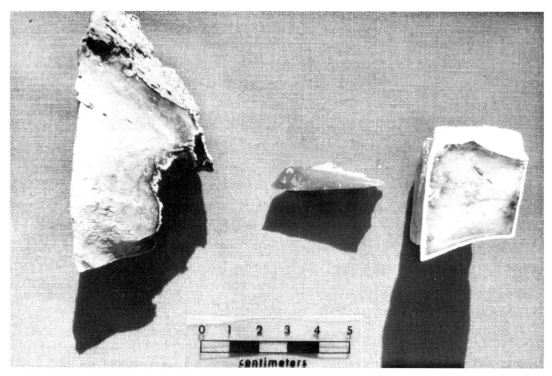

Figure 52. Chert specimens from various depths below surface showing differences in weathering.

Figure 53. Infrared reflection spectra for specimens pictured in figure 52.

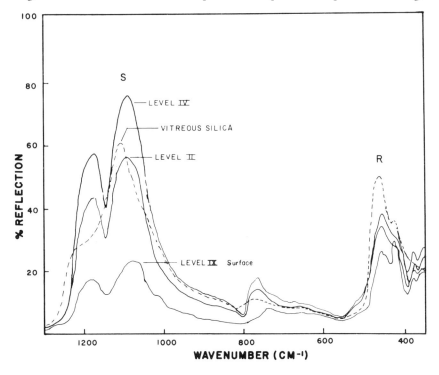

This correlation will be used for calculating the reaction rate constants. Once these constants are determined, the physical properties (such as patina thickness or compositional profile) determined for the field specimens may be used to determine the age of the artifact. For more complete discussions of sample preparation, methodology, and results of these studies see Clark and Purdy (1979*a*, 1979*b*), Purdy and Clark (1979).

The mineralogy, texture, and fabric of a rock reflect its mode of origin. Because it is unlikely that the total environmental conditions under which a rock was formed will be repeated exactly at different times or in different places, similar rock types generally vary (perhaps slightly) if separated by time and distance. Petrographic analysis of stone artifacts, therefore, is potentially valuable to archaeology because geographic sources of archaeological finds might be identified. However, caution is necessary:

> . . . in some instances conditions might be so localized that significant rock changes may occur over a few feet. . . . These differences may be evident in one or more of a variety of ways such as differing grain sizes, varying microstructures, differing minerals and changing chemistry. Notwithstanding this, it will sometimes be that relatively minor differences in rocks will be swamped by major similarities, so that there might be little or no essential difference between rocks originating in widely spaced areas at different times (Sedgley 1970:10).

The factors that determine the physical properties of chert include: (1) the size of the quartz crystals; (2) the habit and mode of aggregation of the crystals; (3) the amount, identity, and distribution of foreign material present (including impurities and fossils); and (4) the number and nature of void spaces. In Florida, there are different types of chert (megascopically) and even a single nodule is not necessarily homogeneous throughout. But, since Florida cherts were formed under generally similar conditions, it may be that cherts from various locations in Florida share common characteristics which may distinguish them from those occurring in other regions. Most cherts from Florida were formed by replacement of carbonate rocks, fossils, or clay by silica, and many of the chert deposits in Florida occur in limestone underlying clay.

In our petrographic analysis, thin sections of chert were prepared to determine whether there are significant differences in flints from the same geologic source, or even from different portions of the same nodule. If so, it might be possible to ascertain if there was differential selection of raw material by native knappers because of its chipping quality.

In addition, thin sections were prepared to determine whether there are significant variations in chert samples from different locations in Florida. This information might be used, in conjunction with other techniques, to establish the source quarries of stone tools and chipping debris recovered from archaeological sites. It might also be used to demonstrate that certain quarries were exploited more frequently because of the superior quality of their stone.

Figure 54 *a-e* shows photomicrographs of several cherts, all of which are broadly similar, from various locations in Florida:

a. Outer portion of a chert nodule from a quarry site near Johnson Lake, Marion County, Florida. Plain light (*left*) and crossed polars (*right*).

b. Inner portion of the chert nodule described above. Morphologically these specimens are dissimilar. The inner portion has a grayish color and texture whereas the outer portion has a brownish color and glassy appearance. Very little difference of any kind (other than iron oxide stains around opaque grains) is observable petrographically. Atomic spectrophotometric analysis, however, did reveal some variations in the proportions of the elements present. Whether or not these variations are significant with regard to chipping quality needs to be investigated further. The quartz is microcrystalline (about .01 mm), and there are abundant patches and spherulites of chalcedony. Crossed polars.

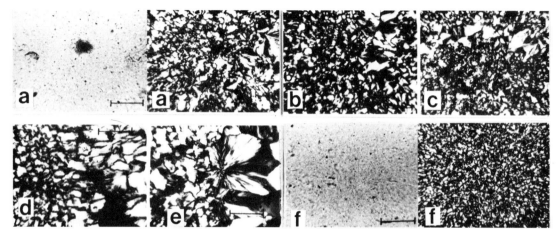

Figure 54. Photomicrographs of Florida cherts and English flint: *(a-c,e)* Marion County, *(d)* Alachua County, *(f)* English flint. All have crossed polars except *a (left)* and *f (left)*, which are plain light.

c. Chert from a quarry site near Johnson Lake, Marion County,
   Florida. This sample came from the same area but from a
   different nodule from that described in *a* and *b* above.
   Microcrystalline quartz (about .01 mm) and chalcedony are
   present. Opaque material is mostly yellowish-brownish in
   reflected light. Crossed polars.

d. Chert from a quarry source in Alachua County, Florida (York's
   property). The chert is composed of microcrystalline quartz
   (about .01 to .02 mm) with pockets of chalcedony. Some fossils
   are present. Crossed polars.

e. Chert from Marion County, Florida showing microcrystalline
   quartz (about .02 mm) and pockets and streaks of spherulitic
   chalcedony (1.5 to 8 μm across). In places the quartz is
   microcrystalline to cryptocrystalline (about .005 mm) and has a
   felted pattern.

In contrast, figure 54f (*left* and *right*) shows chert from England that is microcrystalline to cryptocrystalline quartz (about .005 mm) with small relicts of carbonate. Thin sections of chert from numerous other geographic areas were also examined.

All of the thin sections of cherts from various areas in Florida appear to be broadly similar to each other but are generally dissimilar to cherts from other regions. This suggests the tentative conclusion that, while it may not be possible to determine by petrography the specific location in Florida from which the material of an artifact was obtained, it may be possible to recognize certain artifacts as imported and in some instances it may be possible to suggest a probable or possible source area.

To substantiate further the above conclusions will require intensive examination of many thin sections of samples of chert from the same geologic and geographic source as well as extensive study of cherts from a large number of different geologic and geographic sites (Purdy and Blanchard 1973).

Discussion

The techniques described in this chapter are only a few of those available that can be applied to the study of prehistoric artifacts. It may seem that the methods described are too complex and time-consuming to justify their use. Their use is justified, however, if one considers that the results add new dimensions to archaeological research and that they can be used to supply missing pieces to the prehistoric puzzle. I firmly believe that in the future archaeologists will place greater emphasis upon instrumental investigatory techniques and increased cooperation with colleagues in the physical sciences.

Statistical methods have been of great value to the archaeologist in ordering mind-boggling amounts of data and in pointing out relationships otherwise difficult or impossible to detect or define. At the University of Florida we are compiling data to be computer programmed and statistically analyzed (fig. 18).

Epilogue

Silica from siliceous clays of the Miocene replaced limestones of the Eocene, Oligocene, and Miocene ages to produce the chert sources in Florida. These cherts provided prehistoric stoneworkers with raw material to fashion their tools (map 6). Although chipped stone tool manufacture was only one activity engaged in by early Floridians, stone tool utilization permeated many aspects of culture. Since stone is often the only material preserved from the past in quantity and variety, a study of chert implements provides an important means of understanding past human activities (table 5). Valuable lessons about people and their culture can be learned by reflecting upon two million years of stoneworking technology.

With regard to culture change, it is generally assumed that longstanding pervasive traditions will resist innovation. For instance, it is a widespread belief that when metallurgy developed the switch from tools of stone to those of metal took thousands of years. In Europe it is true that complete cultural integration was not reached until after the Middle Ages, but the seeming lag there between invention and acceptance was probably more a function of the slow development of metallurgical techniques, which caused metals to be expensive and rare, rather than a lack of recognition of their advantages. Stone tool production declined almost immediately among native populations when metal-using Europeans invaded Indians lands during the sixteenth century. The native inhabitants often captured and stripped the invader's ships of all their metal, which they then fashioned into weapons.

History demonstrates that people sometimes will willingly accept

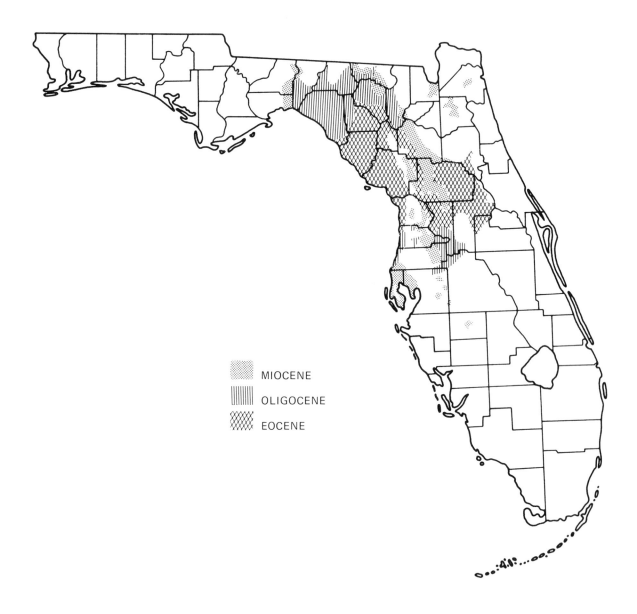

MIOCENE
OLIGOCENE
EOCENE

Map 6. Distribution of Outcrops Probably Containing Chert in Peninsular Florida (adapted from Cook 1945, Plate 1; Brooks, unpublished geologic map of Florida).

Table 5
Evaluating processes of manufacture and modes of utilization

Processes of manufacture

Quarry

Examine geologic-geographic locations for: Proximity to campsites, Time of exploitation (seasonal?)	Determine procurement techniques	Examine debitage for activities at quarries other than stone procurement (woodworking?)	Determine time periods of utilization by: Stylistic differences, Variation in manufacturing techniques, Differences in weathering, Depth below surface

Raw material selection

Determine physical, chemical, and structural properties	Determine whether local or imported	Determine quality

Reduction techniques

Methods	Mechanics	Percussers	Thermal alteration
Pressure, percussion, indirect percussion, or combinations	Direction, force, velocity, angle of blow	Stone, wood, bone	Facilitates flaking and leaves a sharper edge than unaltered chert

Flake morphology

Type of Fracture	Bulb of force	Platform	Size	Shape
Feathered Hinge Step Lateral snap Potlid (or other heat fracture)	Salient Diffuse	Unprepared Prepared	Length Width Thickness Weight	Blade Flake (shaping, thinning)

Use

Scraping   Pounding   Piercing   Cutting

All help determine:
Typologies
Cultural activities
Cultural dynamics

change. The introduction of the horse into Plains Indian culture and the automobile into United States culture are two often-cited examples of profound change that can occur rapidly and permeate all aspects of the social network. The abandonment of stoneworking technology is a third example. In order for changes like these to occur, the people must first be prepared to consider an innovation seriously because they perceive a need for it and, second, resources must be available.

Even though metal implements have replaced stone implements in nearly all areas of the world today, the development of techniques associated with stoneworking laid foundations that developed into such modern-day industries as quarrying and mining. It is especially informative to consider the ramifications of thermal alteration, since the control of fire and the refinement of methods for shaping stone into implements were two of mankind's earliest technologies. The successful application of heat to alter siliceous materials must represent thousands of years of accumulated knowledge.

The benefits that heat treatment conferred to stone implements (and the opportunities it bequeathed to archaeological researchers) are only a small part of the overall significance of thermal alteration. It is possible that metallurgical techniques would not have been developed or would have been delayed if sufficient control of heat had not previously been attained, permitting the extraction of metals from ores. Nor would there have been a ceramic industry because the lessons learned from thermal alteration of silica minerals was a vital prerequisite. It is interesting to note that essentially the same change occurs when clays are fired as when chert is heated, fluxing takes place when the eutectic development is reached.

Often heat-treated chert materials are a different color from the parent stone. Whereas in stone tool production this color change is merely a side effect, in gemstones color change might be very desirable. The steps involved in heating gemstones to induce color change is probably identical to those used to alter stone materials.

144

Carnelian agate, amethyst, spodumenes, and smoky quartz are some examples of gemstones improved by heating.

Turning to a different perspective, the thermoluminescent method was developed to detect the amount of radiation given to cancer patients. The method has since been refined and perfected as a reliable archaeological dating technique by a number of individuals, particularly those working with Martin Aitken at Oxford. A modern-day technique produced in the field of radiological medicine was thus applied to the analysis and study of archaeological specimens.

Laboratory experiments have demonstrated that thermally altered chert materials weather faster than unheated specimens. Although this observation may at first seem to be of only minor interest to archaeologists, it has broader implications. One proposal plan for disposing of high-level nuclear waste materials is to encapsulate them in a boro-silicate matrix to be buried several hundred meters below the surface of the earth. During storage the material will undergo thermal alteration and also be exposed to potentially corrosive environments. Understanding the weathering phenomena of thermally altered artifacts that have been buried for thousands of years may provide a method for predicting long-range corrosion behavior of these encapsulated nuclear waste materials (Purdy 1978; Purdy and Clark 1979).

Our understanding of the evolution of culture generally is enhanced by studies of the evolution of cultural components. A basic component of culture was the technology of stone tool production. Many techniques associated with the chipped stone tool industry have now been transferred to other products of our material culture and, in fact, may have been essential to their development.

Glossary

blade: a cutting tool that is at least twice as long as it is wide and made by the prepared core technique

burin: a prehistoric flint tool with a beveled point

bulb of force: a cone resulting from the spread of force from a knapper's blow

CCA site: Container Corporation of America, Marion County, Florida

chert: a flint rock that contains microscopic quartz particles

chip: a thin flat flake struck from a larger piece of stone

cone: a clamshell shaped peak produced by the fracture of a brittle substance

core: stone raw material with scars showing areas from which flakes have been detached

cortex: the weathered surface or rind of a chert nodule

crutch: a wooden support for the knapper's chest or shoulder sometimes used when detaching blades

debitage: lithic wastes left from toolmaking

flake: an intentionally detached, relatively flat stone chip

fracture: an intentional or nonintentional break

    feathered fracture: a technique to remove flakes with thin, translucent edges

    hinge fracture: flakes with a rounded break opposite the point of impact

    lateral snap fracture: an unintentional break when a tool undergoing knapping separates prematurely and unintentionally from the core, leaving a right angle surface

    step fracture: flakes showing a right angle break opposite the point of impact

graver: a stone tool used to incise

haft: a handle

hafting material: resin or bindings used to secure a tool to a bone or wood handle

hammerstone: a stone tool used for pounding

knapper: a stoneworker

Glossary

material culture: the aggregate of society's physical objects or artifacts

metate: a grindstone

microlith: a small specific purpose tool

microtools: small shaped tools often used in a composite implement

Mousterian period: a Middle Paleolithic period associated with Neanderthal population 40,000–100,000 years ago, principally in Western Europe

Mousterian technique: prepared core

plane: a tool used to smooth a wood surface

prehistory: the history of mankind during the period before recorded events—prior to about 500 years ago in North America

prepared platform: a preliminary surface formed by the knapper to permit him to excert force at the exact angle to remove a desired flake

projectile point: a stone tip attached to a spear, dart, or arrow

reduction: shaping and thinning by removal of flakes from the source material

scraper: a tool used to remove excess material from wood or bone by repeated strokes or to soften hides

Bibliography

Ackerly, Neal W.

    1978   Controlling Pressure in Experimental Lithic Research. *American Antiquity* 43:480-81.

Bennett, Charles E.

    1964   *Laudonnière and Fort Caroline: History and Documents.* Gainesville: University of Florida Press.

    1968   *Settlement of Florida.* Gainesville: University of Florida Press.

Bonnichsen, Robson.

    1977   Models for Deriving Cultural Information from Stone Tools. *Archaeological Survey of Canada,* no. 60. Ottawa.

Bordaz, Jacques.

    1969   Flint Flaking in Turkey. *Natural History* 78:73-79.

    1970   *Tools of the Old and New Stone Age.* Garden City, New York: The Natural History Press.

Bordes, François.

    1968   *The Old Stone Age.* New York: McGraw-Hill.

    1969a   Reflections on Typology and Technique in the Paleolithic. *Arctic Anthropology* 6:1-29.

    1969b   Traitment Thermique du Silex au Solutréen. *Bulletin de la Société Préhistorique Françoise* 66:197.

Bordes, François, and Crabtree, Don E.

    1969   The Corbiac Blade Technique and Other Experiments. *Tebiwa* 12:1-21. Pocatello: Idaho State University.

Bosch, Peter W.

    1979   A Neolithic Flint Mine. *Scientific American* 240:126-32.

Bradley, Bruce.

    1978   Hard Hammer—Soft Hammer: An Alternative Explanation. *Flint Knappers' Exchange* 1:8-10.

Bibliography

Broyles, Bettye J.

    1968   St. Albans Archaic Site, West Virginia. *West Virginia Geological Survey Newsletter* no. 11, p. 11.

    1971   *Second Preliminary Report: The St. Albans Site, Kanawha County, West Virginia.* Report of Archaeological Investigations, no. 3. West Virginia Geological and Economic Survey. Morgantown.

Bryan, Kirk

    1950   *Flint Quarries: The Sources of Tools and, at the Same Time, the Factories of the American Indian.* Papers of the Peabody Museum of American Archaeology and Ethnology 17, no. 3. Cambridge: Harvard University.

Bullen, Adelaide K., and Bullen, Ripley P.

    1950   The Johns Island Site, Hernando County, Florida. *American Antiquity* 12:23-45.

    1974   Further Notes of the West Bay Site. *Florida Anthropologist* 27:119.

Bullen, Ripley P.

    1955   Stratigraphic tests at Blufton, Volusia County, Florida. *Florida Anthropologist* 8:1-16.

    1958   *The Bolen Bluff Site on Paynes Prairie, Florida.* Contributions of the Florida State Museum, Social Sciences, no. 4. Gainesville: University of Florida.

    1969   *Excavations at Sunday Bluff, Florida.* Contributions of the Florida State Museum, Social Sciences, no. 15. Gainesville: University of Florida.

    1972   *The Orange Period of Peninsular Florida.* Florida Anthropological Society Publication, no. 6. Edited by Ripley P. Bullen and James B. Stoltman. *Florida Anthrologist* 25:9-33.

    1975   *A Guide to the Identification of Florida Projectile Points.* 2d ed. Gainesville: Kendall Books.

Bullen, Ripley P., and Beilman, Laurence E.

    1973   The Nalcrest Site, Lake Weohyakapka, Florida. *Florida Anthropologist* 26:1-22.

Bullen, Ripley P., and Dolan, Edward M.

    1959   The Johnson Lake Site, Marion County, Florida. *Florida Anthropologist* 12:77-99.

Bullen, Ripley P., and Wing, Marjorie H.

    1968   A Scraper with Graver Spurs. *Florida Anthropologist* 21:94.

Byers, Douglas S.

    1954   Bull Brook—A Fluted Point Site in Ipswich, Massachusetts. *American Antiquity* 19:343-51.

    1962   Comments. The Paleo Indian Tradition in Eastern North America. *Current Anthropology* 3:247.

Bibliography

Cambron, James W., and Hulse, David C.

    1973   *Handbook of Alabama Archaeology, Part II, Uniface Blade and Flake Tools.*
            Edited by David L. DeJarnette. Birmingham: Cambron.

Cameron, J.R.; Sunthanaligam, N.; and Kenney, G.N.

    1968   *Thermoluminescent Dosimetry.* Madison: University of Wisconsin Press.

Chapman, Jefferson

    1975   *The Rose Island Site and the Bifurcate Point Tradition.* Report of
            Investigations, no. 14. Knoxville: University of Tennessee.

Clark, David E., and Purdy, Barbara A.

    1979a   Electron Microprobe Analysis of Weathered Florida Chert. *American
             Antiquity* 44:517-24.

    1979b   Instrumental Approach to Dating Weathered Florida Chert. *Proceedings of
             the Symposium on Archaeometry and Archaeological Prospection,* pp. 428-39.
             Bonn, Germany.

Clark, D.E.; Acree, W.A.; and Hench, L.L.

    1976   Electron Microprobe Analysis of Coroded Soda-Lime-Silica Glasses.
            Journal of the American Ceramic Society 59:463-64.

Clark, D.E.; Pantano, C.G. Jr.; and Hench, L.L.

    1978   *Glass Corrosion.* New York: Glass Industry Corporation.

Clark, D.E.; Pantano, C.G. Jr.; and Onoda, G.Y. Jr.

    1975   Auger Analysis of Brass-Enamel and Stainless Steel-Enamel Interfaces.
            Journal of the American Ceramic Society 58:336-37.

Clark, D.E.; Dilmore, M.F.; Ethridge, E.C.; and Hench, L.L.

    1976   Aqueous Corrosion of Soda and Soda-Lime-Silica Glass. *Journal of the
            American Ceramic Society* 59:62-65.

Clark, D.E.; Ethridge, E.C.; Dilmore, M.F.; and Hench, L.L.

    1977   Quantitative Analysis of Corroded Glass Using Infrared Frequency Shifts.
            Glass Technology 18:121-24.

Clarke, Rainbird.

    1935   The Flint-Knapping Industry at Brandon. *Antiquity* 9:38-56.

Clausen, Carl J.

    1964   The A-356 Site and the Florida Archaic. Master's thesis, University of
            Florida.

Coe, Joffre Lanning.

    1964   The Formative Cultures of the Carolina Piedmont. *Transactions of the
            American Philosophical Society* 54, pt. 5.

Connor, Jeannette Thurber, trans.

    1964   *Pedro Menéndez de Avilés: Memorial by Gonzalo Solís de Merás.* A facsimile
            reproduction. Gainesville: University of Florida Press.

Bibliography

Crabtree, Don E.

    1966   A Stoneworker's Approach to Analyzing and Replicating the Lindenmeier Folsom. *Tebiwa* 9:3-39.

    1968   Mesoamerican Polyhedral Cores and Prismatic Blades. *American Antiquity* 33:446-78.

    1970   Flaking Stone with Wooden Implements. *Science* 169:146-53.

    1972   *An Introduction to Flintworking: Part I. An Introduction to the Technology of Stone Tools.* Occasional Papers of the Idaho State University, no. 28. Pocatello.

Crabtree, Don E., and Butler, B.R.

    1964   Notes on Experiments in Flint-Knapping: I. Heat Treatment of Silica Minerals. *Tebiwa* 7:1-6.

Crabtree, Don E., and Davis, E.L.

    1968   Experimental Manufacture of Wooden Implements with Tools of Flaked Stone. *Science* 159:426-28.

Cumbaa, Stephen L.

    1973   Aboriginal Use of Marine Mammals in the Southeastern United States. Paper presented at the 30th Southeastern Archaeological Conference. Memphis, Tennessee.

DeJarnette, David L.; Kurjack, Edward B.; and Cambron, James W.

    1962   Stanfield-Worley Bluff Shelter Excavation. *Journal of Alabama Archaeology* 8, nos. 1 & 2.

Dubois, Cora.

    1935   *Wintu Ethnography.* University of California Publications in American Archaeology and Ethnology, 36:127. Berkeley.

Ellis, H. Holmes.

    1940   *Flint-working Techniques of the American Indians: An Experimental Study.* Columbus: The Ohio Historical Society Publication, no. 72.

Fairbanks, Charles H.

    1959   Additional Elliots Point Complex Sites. *Florida Anthropologist* 12:95-100.

Faulkner, Alaric.

    1972   Mechanical Principles of Flint Working, Ph.D. dissertation, Washington State University. Pullman.

Florida State Board of Conservation.

    1939   *Aboriginal Stone Quarries of Hillsborough County and Sources of Abrasions and Pigment.* Third Biennial Report.

Gallagher, James P.

    1977   Contemporary Stone Tools in Ethiopia: Implications for Archaeology. *Journal of Field Archaeology* 4:407-14.

Bibliography

Gardner, William M., ed.

1974   *The Flint Run Paleo-Indian Complex, A Preliminary Report, 1971-73 Seasons.* Occasional Publications no. 1, Department of Anthropology. Washington: The Catholic University of America.

Goggin, John M.

1950   An Early Lithic Complex From Central Florida. *American Antiquity* 16:46-49.

Goodwin, A.J.H.

1961   Chemical Alteration (Patination of Stone). *The Application of Quantitative Methods in Archaeology.* Edited by Robert F. Heizer and Sherburne F. Cook. Viking Fund Publications in Anthropology, no. 28:300-24. Chicago: Quadrangle Books.

Goodyear, Albert C.

1973   Archaic Hafted Spokeshaves with Graver Spurs from the Southeast. *Florida Anthropologist* 26:39-44.

1974   *The Brand Site: A Techno-Functional Study of a Dalton Site in Northeast Arkansas.* Arkansas Archaeological Survey Research Series, no. 7. Fayetteville, Arkansas: University of Arkansas Museum.

Goodyear, Albert C.; Thompson, William; and Warren, Lyman O.

1968   Suwannee Style End Scrapers from Pinellas County. *Florida Anthropologist* 21:91.

Gould, R.A.

1968   Chipping Stones in the Outback. *Natural History* 77:42-49.

Gould, Richard A.; Koster, Dorothy A.; and Sontz, Ann H.L.

1971   The Lithic Assemblage of the Western Desert Aborigines of Australia. *American Antiquity* 36:149-69.

Griffin, John W.

1974   *Investigations in Russell Cave.* Publications in Archaeology, no. 13. Washington: National Park Service.

Haag, William G., and Webb, Clarence H.

1953   Microblades at Poverty Point Sites. *American Antiquity* 18:245-48.

Haisten, James M.

1974   Two Crooked Creek Nonceramic Sites. *Florida Anthropologist* 27:125-32.

Heizer, R.F., and Treganza, A.E.

1944   Mines and Quarries of the Indians of California. *California Journal of Mines and Geology* 40:291–359.

Hemmings, E. Thomas.

1975   The Silver Springs Site, Prehistory in the Silver Springs Valley, Florida. *Florida Anthropologist* 28:141-58.

153

Bibliography

Hemmings, E. Thomas, and Kohler, Timothy A.

    1974   *The Lake Kanapaha Site in North Central Florida,* Bulletin 4. Tallahassee: Bureau of Historic Sites and Properties.

Hench, L.L., and Clark, D.E.

    1978   Physical Chemistry of Glass Surfaces. *Journal of Non-Crystalline Solids.*

Hester, Thomas R.

    1972   Ethnographic Evidence for the Thermal Alteration of Siliceous Stone. *Tebiwa* 15:63-65.

Hester, Thomas R., and Heizer, Robert F.

    1973   *Bibliography of Archaeology I: Experiments, Lithic Technology and Petrography.* Module in Anthropology, no. 29:1-56. Reading, Mass: Addison-Wesley.

Hester, Thomas R.; Delbert, Gilbow; and Albee, Alan D.

    1973   A Functional Analysis of "Clearfork" Artifacts from the Rio Grande Plain, Texas. *American Antiquity* 38:90-96.

Hole, Frank, and Heizer, Robert F.

    1973   *An Introduction to Prehistoric Archaeology.* 3d ed. New York: Holt, Rinehart and Winston.

Holmes, W.H.

    1919   *Handbook of Aboriginal American Antiquities. Part 1. Introductory—The Lithic Industries.* Bureau of American Ethnology, Bulletin 60. Washington: The Smithsonian Institution.

Katz, Paul, and Katz, Susanna.

    1975   A Lithic Analysis of the Settlement Pattern in the Lower Tule Canyon, Brescoe County, Texas. Paper presented to the Society of American Archaeology. Dallas, Texas.

Kerkhof, Von Frank and Muller-Beck, Hansjurgen.

    1969   Zur Brachmechanischen Deutung der Schlagmarken an Steingeraten. *Glastechnische Berichte,* 42 Jahrg, Haft 10:439-48.

Kingery, W.D.

    1960   *Introduction to Ceramics.* New York: Wiley.

Knight, James D.

    1976   Manufacturing Techniques of Maximo Point Microliths. *Florida Anthropologist* 29:84-92.

Knowles, Sir Francis H.S.

    1944   *The Manufacture of a Flint Arrow-head by Quartzite Hammer-stone.* Occasional Papers on Technology, no. 1. Pitt Rivers Museum, Oxford: University Press.

    1953   *Stone-Worker's Progress: A Study of Stone Implements in the Pitt Rivers Museum.* Occasional Papers on Technology, no. 6. Oxford: University Press.

154

Kroeber, Theodora.

    1961   *Ishi in Two Worlds.* Berkeley: University of California Press.

Laudonnière, Rene.

    1975   *Three Voyages.* Translated by Charles E. Bennett. Gainesville: The University Presses of Florida.

Lazarus, William C.

    1958   A Poverty Point Complex in Florida. *Florida Anthropologist* 11:23-32.

Leaky, Mary D.

    1971   *Olduvai Gorge: 3. Excavation in Beds 1 & 2, 1960-1963.* Cambridge University Press.

Lewis, Thomas M.N., and Lewis, Madeleine Knebert.

    1961   *Eva, An Archaic Site.* Knoxville: University of Tennessee Press.

Luedtke, Barbara E.

    1978   The Identification of Sources of Chert Artifacts. Paper presented at the 43d Annual Meeting of the Society for American Antiquity. Tucson, Arizona.

McCary, Ben C.

    1951   A Workshop Site of Early Man in Dinwiddie County, Virginia. *American Antiquity* 17:9-17.

MacDonald, George F.

    1968   *Debert: A Palaeo-Indian Site in Central Nova Scotia.* Anthropology Papers, no. 16. Ottawa: National Museum of Canada.

Markham, Clements R., ed.

    1878   *The Hawkins' Voyages.* London: Hakluyt Society.

Mason, Ronald J.

    1962   The Paleo-Indian Tradition in Eastern North America. *Current Anthropology* 3:227-78.

Mewhinney, H.

    1957   *A Manual for Neanderthals.* Austin: University of Texas Press.

Michael, Henry N., and Ralph, Elizabeth K.

    1971   *Dating Techniques for the Archaeologist.* Cambridge: MIT Press.

Michels, Joseph W.

    1967   Archaeology and Dating by Hydration of Obsidian. *Science* 158:211–14.

Michie, James L.

    1968   The Edgefield Scraper. *The Chesopiean* 6:30-31.

    1973   The Edgefield Scraper: Its Inferred Antiquity and Use. *The Chesopiean* 11:2-10.

155

Bibliography

Mock, Donald R.

    1978   Proton Induced X-Ray Emission Analysis of Peninsular Florida Cherts. Master's thesis, University of Florida.

Morse, Dan F.

    1973   Dalton Culture in Northeast Arkansas. *Florida Anthropologist* 26:23-38.

Morse, Dan F., and Tesar, Louis D.

    1974   A Microlithic Tool Assemblage from a Northwest Florida Site. *Florida Anthropologist* 27:89-106.

Movius, Hallam L., Jr.; David, Nicholas C.; Bricker, Harvey M.; and Clay, R. Berle.

    1968   *The Analysis of Certain Major Classes of Upper Palaeolithic Tools.* Edited by Hugh Hencken. Peabody American School of Prehistoric Research, Bulletin 26. Cambridge, Mass: Peabody Museum.

Munsell, A.H.

    1946   *A Color Notation.* 10th ed. Baltimore, Maryland: Munsell Color Co.

Neill, Wilfred T.

    1971   A Florida Paleo-Indian Implement of Ground Stone. *Florida Anthropologist* 24:61-70.

Nevin, Charles M.

    1942   *Principles of Structural Geology.* 3d ed. London: Wiley.

Oakley, Kenneth P.

    1972   *Man, The Tool-maker.* 6th ed. London: The Trustees of the British Museum.

Pirkle, E.C.

    1956   The Hawthorne and Alachua Formations of Alachua County, Florida. *Quarterly Journal of the Florida Academy of Sciences* 19:197-240.

Pope, Saxton T.

    1918   *Yahi Archery.* University of California Publications in American Archaeology and Ethnology, 13:103-52. Berkeley.

Preston, F.W.

    1926   A Study of the Rupture of Glass. *Journal of the Society of Glass Technology* 10:234-69.

Purdy, Barbara A.

    1971a   The Importance of Quarry Sites. *Science and Archaeology* 8:5-6.

    1971b   Investigations Concerning the Thermal Alteration of Silica Minerals: An Archaeological Approach. Ph.D. dissertation, University of Florida.

    1974   Investigations Concerning the Thermal Alteration of Silica Minerals: An Archaeological Approach. *Tebiwa* 17:37-66.

1975a The Senator Edwards Chipped Stone Workshop Site (8-MR-122), Marion County, Florida: A Preliminary Report of Investigations. *Florida Anthropologist* 28:178-89.

1975b Fractures for the Archaeologist. *Lithic Technology: Making and Using Stone Tools.* Edited by Earl Swanson. Chicago: Aldine Press.

1976 The Application of Instrumental Techniques to Prehistoric Remains of Florida. *Lithic Technology* 5:5-6.

1977 The York Site (8-A1-480), Alachua County, Florida: Observations on Aboriginal Use of Chert. *Florida Anthropologist* 30:3-8.

1981a An Investigation into the Use of Chert Outcrops by Prehistoric Floridians. *Florida Anthropologist,* in press.

1981b Pyrotechnology: Prehistoric Applications to Chert Materials in North America. *Early Pyrotechnology.* Washington: The Smithsonian Institution.

n.d. The Hendrix Scraper: A Paleo Indian Tool in Florida. In preparation.

n.d. The Waller Hafted Scraper-Knife: An Early Stone Implement in Florida. In preparation.

Purdy, Barbara A., and Beach, Laurie.

1980 The Chipped Stone Tool Industry of Florida's Preceramic Archaic. *Archaeology of Eastern North America.* 8:105-124.

Purdy, Barbara A., and Blanchard, Frank N.

1973 Petrography as a Means of Tracing Stone Tools from Florida. *Florida Anthropologist* 26:121-25.

Purdy, Barbara A., and Brooks, H.K.

1971 Thermal Alteration of Silica Minerals: An Archaeological Approach. *Science* 173:322-25.

Purdy, Barbara A., and Clark, David E.

1979 Weathering Studies of Chert: A Potential Solution to the Chronology Problem in Florida, pp. 440-50. *Proceedings of the Symposium of Archaeometry and Archaeological Prospection.* Bonn, Germany.

Purdy, Barbara A., and Roessler, Genevieve S.

n.d. Neutron Activation Analysis of Florida Chert. In preparation.

Purdy, Barbara A.; Clark, D.E.; and Maurer, Christopher.

1980 Investigation of an Early Lithic Industry in Florida. Proposal submitted to National Science Foundation.

Reichelt, David C.

1974 Microliths of South Walton County. *Florida Anthropologist* 27:120-24.

Bibliography

Renfrew, Colin.

    1978   Trajectory Discontinuity and Morphogenesis. The Implications of Catastrophe Theory of Archaeology. *American Antiquity* 43:203-222.

Ribault, Jean.

    1964   *The Whole and True Discovery of Terra Florida.* A Facsimile Reprint of the London Edition of 1563. Gainesville: University of Florida Press.

Ritchie, William A.

    1953   A Probable Paleo-Indian Site in Vermont. *American Antiquity* 18:249-58.

Roberts, Frank H.H., Jr.

    1936   *Additional Information on the Folsom Complex.* Smithsonian Miscellaneous Collections 95, no. 10. Washington.

Robertson, James A., trans. and ed.

    1932   *True Relation of the Hardships Suffered by Governor Hernando de Soto and Certain Portuguese Gentlemen During the Discovery of the Province of Florida: Now newly set forth by a Gentlemen of Elvas.* 2 vols. Deland, Florida: Florida State Historical Society.

Sanders, D.M.; Person, W.B.; and Hench, L.L.

    1972   New Methods for Studying Glass Corrosion Kinetics. *Applied Spectroscopy* 26:530-36.

Sedgley, J.

    1970   Some Problems Connected with the Petrographic Examination of Stone Artifacts. *Science and Archaeology* nos. 2 & 3:10-11.

Semenov, S.A.

    1964   *Prehistoric Technology.* London: Cory, Adams, and MacKay.

Sharon, D.W., and Watson, T.C.

    1971   The Two Egg Quarry Site. *Florida Anthropologist* 24:77-80.

Simpson, J. Clarence.

    1941   Source Material for Florida Aboriginal Artifacts. *Proceedings of the Florida Academy of Science* 1940, 5:32-34.

    1948   Folsom-Like Points from Florida. *Florida Anthropologist* 1:11-15.

Singer, Clay A., and Ericson, Jonathan E.

    1977   Quarry Analysis at Bodie Hills, Mono County, California: A Case Study. *Exchange Systems in Prehistory.* New York: Academic Press.

Snyder, J. F.

    1881   *Smithsonian Annual Report,* p. 563. Washington.

Sollberger, J.B.

    1971   A Technological Study of Beveled Knives. *Plains Anthropologist* 16:209-18.

    1978   Craftsman. *Flintknappers' Exchange* 1:16.

Southern Standard Building Code.

    1973   Chapter 16. Concrete Construction. Birmingham, Alabama: Southern Building Code Congress International Inc.

Speth, John D.

    1972   Mechanical Basis of Percussion Flaking. *American Antiquity* 37:34-60.

Stafford, Barbara D.

    1977   Burin Manufacture and Utilization: An Experimental Study. *Journal of Field Archaeology* 4:235-46.

Swanton, John R.

    1946   *The Indians of the Southeastern United States.* Bureau of American Ethnology, Bulletin 137. Washington: The Smithsonian Institution.

Tite, M.S.

    1972   *Methods of Physical Examination in Archaeology.* London: Seminar Press.

Tixier, Jacques.

    1974   Glossary for the Description of Stone Tools. Translated by M.H. Newcomer. *Newsletter of Lithic Technology: Special Publication* no. 1.

Tringham, Ruth; Cooper, G.; Odell, G.; Voylek, B.; and Whitman, A.

    1974   Experimentation in the Formation of Edge Damage: A New Approach to Lithic Analysis. *Journal of Field Archaeology* 1:171-96.

Tugby, Donald J.

    1958   A Typological Analysis of Axes and Choppers from Southeast Australia. *American Antiquity* 24:24-33.

Walker, S.T.

    1879   Indian Mounds in Southern Florida. *Annual Report of the Smithsonian Institution.* Washington.

Waller, Ben I.

    1969   Paleo-Indian and Other Artifacts from a Florida Stream Bed. *Florida Anthropologist* 22:37-39.

    1970   Some Occurrences of Paleo-Indian Projectile Points in Florida Waters. *Florida Anthropologist* 23:129-34.

    1971   Hafted Flake Knives. *Florida Anthropologist* 24:173-74.

Waller, Ben I., and Dunbar, James.

    1977   Distribution of Paleo-Indian Projectiles in Florida. *Florida Anthropologist* 30:79-80.

Warren, Lyman O.

    1973   Unique Knife or Chisel, Piper-Fuller Airfield, St. Petersburg. *Florida Anthropologist* 26:119-20.

Watson, Thomas C.

    1974   The Microlithic West Bay Site, Florida. *Florida Anthropologist* 27:107-18.

Bibliography

Watson, William.

    1968   *Flint Implements: An Account of Stone Age Techniques and Cultures.* London: The Trustees of the British Museum.

White, Peter J.

    1967   Ethno-Archaeology in New Guinea, Two Examples. *Mankind* 6:409-14.

Willey, Gordon R.

    1949   *Archaeology of the Florida Gulf Coast.* Smithsonian Miscellaneous Collections, 113. Washington.

Wilmsen, Edwin.

    1970   *Lithic Analysis and Cultural Inference: A Paleo-Indian Case.* Anthropological Papers of the University of Arizona, no. 16. Tucson.

Witthoft, John.

    1952   A Paleo Indian Site in Eastern Pennsylvania: An Early Hunting Culture. *Proceedings, American Philosophical Society* 96:464-95.

    1968   Lithic Materials and Technology. *Southeastern Archaeological Conference Bulletin,* 9:3-18.

Wormington, H.M.

    1957   *Ancient Man in North America.* 4th rev. ed. The Denver Museum of Natural History Popular Series, no. 4

Zimmerman, David W.

    1978   Thermoluminescence: A Dating and Authenticating Method for Art Objects. *Technology and Conservation* 3:32-37.

Index

Index

Index

Index